BRANCH LINES AROUND OSWESTRY

Vic Mitchell and Keith Smith

MP Middleton Press

Front cover: The headquarters of the Cambrian Railways form the background on 1st July 1961 as no. 7802 Bradley Manor *waits to leave Oswestry with the 4.10pm Whitchurch to Welshpool train. The locomotive was built in 1938. (L.W.Rowe)*

Back cover: Oswestry became home of the Cambrian Railways Society in 1972 and visiting on 8th June 2002 was ex-GWR no. 7822 Foxcote Manor. *(T.Heavyside)*

Published October 2009
First reprint May 2015

ISBN 978 1 906008 60 4

© *Middleton Press, 2009*

Design Deborah Esher

Published by
> *Middleton Press*
> *Easebourne Lane*
> *Midhurst*
> *West Sussex*
> *GU29 9AZ*
Tel: 01730 813169
Fax: 01730 812601
Email: info@middletonpress.co.uk
www.middletonpress.co.uk

Printed in the United Kingdom by IJ Graphics, Guildford, Surrey. GU4 7WA

CONTENTS

INDEX

ACKNOWLEDGEMENTS

We are very grateful for the assistance received from many of those mentioned in the credits also to P.G.Barnes, A.R.Carder, L.Crosier, G.Croughton, J.B.Horne, S.C.Jenkins, N.Langridge, B.Lewis, D.H.Mitchell, P.Motram, A.Rhodes, D.T.Rowe, Mr D. and Dr S.Salter, and in particular, our always supportive wives, Barbara Mitchell and Janet Smith.

I. The GWR map for 1948 has its main lines shown with broad lines.

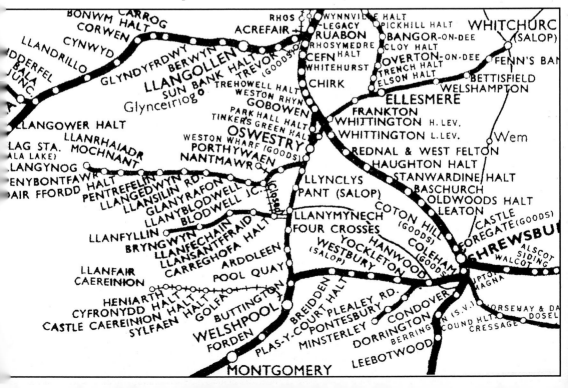

GEOGRAPHICAL SETTING

We start our journey south at Gobowen, which is close to the once productive coal measures that stretched north through Flintshire. The ground west of Oswestry rises steeply to the peaks of Berwyn, but our route south descends gently from this old market town into the Severn Valley, near Pool Quay and follows the River Severn to Welshpool.

A tributary passes close to Llanymynech and this is the River Vyrnwy. West of this place, two rivers flow from the west into it: the Afon Tanat and, south of it, the Afon Cain. The branch to Llangynog followed the former and was thus known locally as the Tanat Valley Railway; the line to Llanfyllin was close to the latter.

The geology varies from east to west and of economic importance is a long outcrop of limestone, which was conveyed by rail almost to the end of the 20th century, from quarries west of Llynclys.

North of Llanymynech the line was built in Shropshire and south thereof in Montgomeryshire, thus we travel from England into Wales. Part of the TVR passed through the southern tip of Denbighshire.

The maps are to the scale of 25ins to 1 mile, with north at the top, unless otherwise indicated.

Welsh spelling and hyphenation have varied over the years and so we have generally used the most recent form, as have the railways.

II. The 1946 edition is at approximately 4 miles to 1 inch.

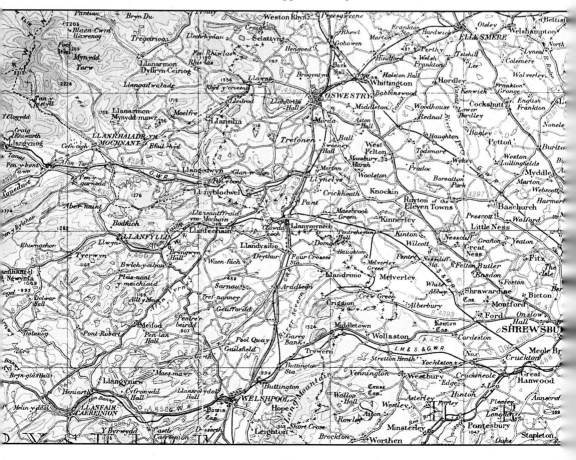

HISTORICAL BACKGROUND

Trains of the Shrewsbury & Chester Railway began running through Gobowen in 1848 and its short branch from there to Oswestry came into use on 1st January 1849. The Oswestry & Newtown Railway opened south to Welshpool on 1st May 1860 and on to Newtown the next year. It became part of the Cambrian Railways in 1864, the year in which the line from Ellesmere to Oswestry opened. The O&NR had opened its branch from Llanymynech to Llanfyllin in July 1863. The former was reached by the Potteries, Shrewsbury & North Wales Railway in 1866, but it ran only between Shrewsbury and Nantmawr, about two miles north of Llanymynech.

The Shrewsbury & Welshpool Railway opened between those places in 1862 and became jointly owned by the Great Western Railway and the London & North Western Railway in 1865. The Shrewsbury & Chester had become part of the GWR in 1854. The O&NR completed a short mineral branch west of Llynclys to Porthywaen in 1861. The first mile of this formed the eastern end of the Tanat Valley Light Railway, which opened for passengers to Llangynog on 6th January 1904. It became part of the Cambrian Railways in 1921, which itself was absorbed into the GWR in 1922.

Known as "The Potts", the PS&NWR became simply the Shropshire Railways in 1888, although the section east of Llanymynech was closed from 1880. The part west thereof to Nantmawr was operated by the Cambrian Railways from 1881. The eastern part became the Shropshire & Montgomeryshire Light Railway in 1909 and reopened to Shrewsbury in 1911. It closed to passengers in 1933 and totally in 1960, having been under military control since 1941.

With the advent of nationalisation, all non-Army lines in the area became part of the Western Region of British Railways on 1st January 1948. The routes were transferred to the London Midland Region on 17th June 1963.

Passenger services were withdrawn thus: to Llangynog on 15th January 1951, to Llanfyllin and also Whitchurch-Oswestry-Welshpool on 18th January 1965. The Gobowen-Oswestry branch lasted until 7th November 1966. Freight closures are given in the captions.

PASSENGER SERVICES

Gobowen-Oswestry
The table on the right indicates the number of trains in selected years, southbound.

	Weekdays	Sundays
1870	8	2
1901	24	0
1936	28	0
1944	20	4
1950	25	4
1966	17	0

Oswestry-Welshpool
This formed part of the main line of the Cambrian Railways between Whitchurch and Aberystwyth, many trains running between these places in the early years. Most terminated at Welshpool in the final years.

This section of the route had a remarkably consistent pattern of service, with five weekday trains and one on Sundays in every year examined from 1869, but there were also some short workings for a few years.

Llangynog Branch (Tanat Valley)
The initial timetable showed four trains on weekdays, with extras on certain days, but no services were provided on Sundays, at all. The basic frequency was down to three by 1924 and two upon closure. All trains started at Oswestry.

Llanfyllin Branch
There were four trains on weekdays in the first few years, this increasing to five for most of the life of the line. No references to Sunday activity have been found. Most trains operated from Llanymynech initially and from Oswestry in later years.

GOBOWEN and OSWESTRY.—Great Western.

Mls	Down.	mrn	mrn	mrn	mrn	mrn	mrn	aft	aft	aft	aft	aft	aft	aft	aft	aft	aft	aft	aft	aft	aft	aft	aft	aft	aft	aft
—	Gobowen..dep.	7 10	7 48	9 5	9b18	10 5	1040	12 3	1225	1 20	1 48	2 17	2 45	3c16	3 48	4 30	5 29	5 52	6 11	6 36	7 13	7 22	8 28	9 8	10 5	1040
2¼	Oswestry 380..	7 17	7 55	9 12	9b25	1012	1047	1210	1232	1 27	1 55	2 24	2 52	3c23	3 55	4 37	5 36	5 59	6 18	6 37	7 20	7 30	8 35	9 15	1012	1047
Mls	**Up.**	mrn	mrn	mrn	mrn	mrn	mrn	aft	aft	aft	aft	aft	aft	aft	aft	aft	aft	aft	aft	aft	aft	aft	aft	aft	aft	
—	Oswestry dep.	7 0	7 25	8 40	9 40	1025	1143	1214	1 5	2 0	2 30	3 5	3 30	4 5	4b55	5 8	5 42	6 4	6 22	7 5	8 10	8 45	9 0	9 45	1020	....
2¼	Gobowen 42.	7 7	7 32	8 47	9 47	1032	1150	1221	1 12	2 7	2 37	3 12	3 37	4 12	5b2	5 15	5 49	6 11	6 29	7 12	8 17	8 52	9 7	9 52	1027	....

b Wednesdays only. c Except Wednesdays.

January 1901

OSWESTRY and GOBOWEN.

Miles	Up.	Week Days																															Sn
		mrn m	mn	mrn	mn	mrn	mrn	mrn m	mrn m	aft	aft	aft m	aft	aft	aft	aft m	aft W	aft	aft m	aft	aft S	aft	S m	aft m	aft m	aft m	aft m	aft	aft m	aft	aft m	aft		
—	Oswestry ¶........dep.	7 40	7 50	8 15	9 3	9 45	1012	1025	1153	12 3	1235	1254	1 8	1 55	2 30	2 56	3 10	3 45	4 23	4 40	5 10	5 39	6 30	6 55	7 8	7 38	7 50	8 34	8 45	9 36	9 50	11 0	..	..
2¼	Gobowen 112......arr.	7 48	7 56	8 23	9 11	9 51	1018	1034	12 1	1211	1241	1 2	1 14	2 3	2 39	3 4	3 16	3 54	4 31	4 48	5 18	5 47	6 38	7 3	7 14	7 46	7 58	8 40	8 53	9 44	9 58	11 8	..	..

E Except Sats. m One class only. S Sats. only. W Weds. only.

¶ "Halt" at Park Hall between Oswestry and Gobowen. A Road Motor Service is available on Sundays between Oswestry and Gobowen.

February 1936

Table 158

OSWESTRY and GOBOWEN

Miles		Week Days																					
		a.m 3	a.m		a m	a.m		a.m	a.m 3		a.m	a.m		p.m	p.m 3	p m	p.m	p.m		p.m	p.m	p.m S3	p.m
—	Oswestry..........dep	7 35	7 50	..	8 15	8 47	..	9 47	1017	..	1042	1120	..	12 5	1240	1255	1 18	2 15	..	3 5	3 45	4 7	4 25
1¾	Park Hall Halt..........	7 40	..	..	8 20	8 52	..	9 52	1022	..	1047	1125	..	1210	1245	1 0	..	2 20	..	3 10	3 50	4 12	4 30
2¼	Gobowen..........arr	7 43	7 56	..	8 23	8 55	..	9 55	1025	..	1050	1128	..	1213	1248	1 3	1 24	2 23	..	3 13	3 53	4 15	4 33

	Week Days—continued									Sundays													
	p.m 3	p.m		p.m	p.m 3	p.m 3	p.m 3	p.m 3	p.m		a.m	a.m	a.m	a.m		p.m	p.m	p.m		p.m	p.m	p.m	
Oswestry..........dep	4 45	5 30	..	6 5	7 7	8 15	9 0	9 50	1025	..	9 20	9 47	1050	1125	..	1215	3 25	4 15	..	4 45	6 30	8 30	..
Park Hall Halt..........	4 50	5 35	..	..	7 12	8 20	9 5	9 55	1030	..	9 25	9 52	1055	1130	..	1220	3 30	4 20	..	4 50	6 35	8 35	..
Gobowen..........arr	4 53	5 38	..	6 11	7 15	8 23	9 8	9 58	1033	..	9 28	9 55	1058	1133	..	1223	3 33	4 23	..	4 53	6 38	8 38	..

Miles		Week Days																					
		a.m 3	a.m	a.m		a.m	a.m 3	a.m		a.m	a.m		p.m 3	p.m	p.m	p.m	p.m		p.m	p.m	p.m S3	p.m	p.m 3
—	Gobowen..........dep	7 10	8 7	8 36	..	9 10	9 57	1027	..	1052	1135	..	1215	1230	1 26	1 40	2 50	..	3 30	4 15	4 35	4 55	5 15
¾	Park Hall Halt..........	7 13	8 10	8 39	..	9 13	10 0	1030	..	1055	1138	..	1218	1233	1 29	1 43	2 53	..	3 33	4 18	4 38	4 58	5 18
2¼	Oswestry..........arr	7 18	8 15	8 44	..	9 18	10 5	1035	..	11 0	1143	..	1223	1238	1 34	1 48	2 58	..	3 38	4 23	4 43	5 3	5 23

	Week Days—continued										Sundays												
	p.m	p.m	p.m 3	p.m 3	p.m 3		p.m 3	p.m	p.m		a.m	a.m	a.m	a.m	a.m		p.m	p.m	p.m	p.m	p.m	p.m	
Gobowen..........dep	5 55	6 13	6 32	7 40	8 37	..	8 50	1050	1111	..	6 20	9 37	10 0	1115	1147	..	1240	3 50	4 35	5 2	6 52	8 52	..
Park Hall Halt..........	5 58	..	6 35	7 43	8 40	..	8 53	1053	1114	..	..	9 40	10 3	1118	1150	..	1243	3 53	4 38	5 5	6 55	8 55	..
Oswestry..........arr	6 3	6 19	6 40	7 48	8 45	..	8 58	1058	1119	..	6 26	9 45	10 8	1123	1155	..	1248	3 58	4 43	5 10	7 0	9 0	..

S Saturdays only. 3 Third class only.

June 1950

POTTERIES, SHREWSBURY, and NORTH WALES.

Sec., C. Chandler.] All 1 & 2 class gov. [Gen. Man., J. Bucknall Cooper, Shrewsbury.

Mls	Fares. 1 cl. s. d.	2 cl. s. d.	3 cl. s. d.	Down.	Week Days. a	mrn	aft	aft		Sndys	
—				Abbey Station, Shrewsbury..dep	6 45	9 30	3 5	6 15	....	....	....
3	....	....	....	Red Hill	6 53	9 38	3 13	6 23	....	....	....
4	....	....	....	Hanwood Road...	6 56	9 41	3 16	6 26	....	....	....
7¼	....	....	....	Cross Gates	7 5	9 50	3 25	6 35	....	....	....
9¼	....	....	....	Shrawardine	7 13	9 58	3 33	6 43	....	....	....
11¼	....	....	....	Nesscliff..........	7 20	10 5	3 40	6 50	....	....	....
13½	....	....	....	Kinnerley........	7 25	1010	3 45	6 55	....	....	....
16	....	....	....	Maesbrook	7 31	1015	3 55	7 5	....	....	....
18	....	....	....	Llanymynch { ar	7 38	1020	4 0	7 10	....	....	....
				130, 131 { dp	7 43	1024	4 5	7 13	....	....	....
20½	....	....	....	Llanyblodwell arr	7 53	1034	4 13	7 18	....	....	....

Mls	Up.	Week Days. a	mrn	aft	aft	
—	Llanyblodwell dp	8 0	1033	4 15	7 20	....
2½	Llanymynch { ar	8 5	1038	4 25	7 25	....
	130, 131 { dp	8 15	1055	4 40	7 45	....
4½	Maesbrook	8 22	11 2	4 47	7 52	....
7	Kinnerley	8 30	1110	4 55	8 0	....
9¼	Nesscliff	8 36	1115	5 0	8 5	....
11	Shrawardine	8 41	1120	5 5	8 10	....
13¼	Cross Gates	8 50	1130	5 10	8 15	....
16½	Hanwood Road...	8 56	1140	5 20	8 25	....
17½	Red Hill ....[127	9 2	1143	5 25	8 28	....
20½	Shrewsbury 125,	9 10	1150	5 35	8 35	....

a Run on Weds., Sats., and alternate Tuesdays (Shrewsbury Fair Days). 1, Station for Llangedwyn.

December 1870

OSWESTRY, BLODWEL JUNCTION, and LLANGYNOG—Tanat Valley Light.—Cambrian.

Mls		mrn	mrn	aft (Mons. & Sats.)	aft	aft	
—	Oswestry............dep.	8 25	1115	2 5	3 55	7 45	....
4¾	Porthywaen..............	8 37	1128	2 18	4 8	7 58	....
6	Blodwel Junction ....arr.	8 42	1133	2 23	4 13	8 3	....
—	Mls — Llanymynech....dep.	8 15	....	....	4 0	....	....
—	2½ Blodwel Junction arr.	8 25	....	....	4 10	....	....
—	Blodwel Junction ....dep.	8 43	1135	2 24	4 15	8 4	....
6¾	Llanyblodwel..............	8 48	1140	2 29	4 20	8 9	....
9¼	Llansilin Road..............	9 1	1153	2 42	4 30	8 22	....
10¾	Llangedwyn..............	9 6	1158	2 47	4 38	8 27	....
12¾	Pentrefelin	9 14	12 6	2 55	4 46	8 35	....
14	Llanrhaiadr Mochnant....	9 20	1213	3 2	4 53	8 42	....
15¼	Pedair Ffordd..............	9 25	1218	3 7	4 58	8 47	....
17	Penybontfawr..............	9 32	1226	3 15	5 6	8 55	....
19½	Llangynog ....arr.	9 40	1235	3 25	5 15	9 5	....

Mls		mrn (Wednesdays only.)	aft (Except Wednesdays.)	mrn	aft	aft	aft (Mons. & Sats.)	
—	Llangynog ....dep.	6 50	7 0	9 50	1 35	5 50	7 15	....
2½	Penybontfawr..............	6 58	7 8	9 58	1 43	5 58	7 23	....
4¼	Pedair Ffordd..............	7 5	7 15	10 5	1 50	6 5	7 30	....
5½	Llanrhaiadr Mochnant....	7 10	7 20	1010	1 55	6 10	7 35	....
6¾	Pentrefelin	7 15	7 25	1015	2 0	6 15	7 40	....
8¾	Llangedwyn..............	7 20	7 30	1020	2 5	6 20	7 45	....
10¼	Llansilin Road..............	7 30	7 37	1027	2 12	6 27	7 52	....
12¾	Llanyblodwel..............	7 37	7 44	1034	2 19	6 34	7 59	....
13½	Blodwel Junction ....arr.	7 41	7 48	1038	2 23	6 38	8 3	....
—	Blodwel Junction.dep.	7 55	7 55	1041	2 30	....	....	....
15¼	Llanymynech 398 arr.	8 5	8 5	1050	2 40	....	....	....
—	Blodwel Junction ....dep.	7 45	7 50	1040	2 25	6 40	8 4	....
14¾	Porthywaen..............	7 55	7 56	1045	2 31	6 46	8 11	....
19½	Oswestry 398, 401...arr.	8 10	8 10	11 0	2 45	7 0	8 25	....

July 1904

OSWESTRY, BLODWELL JUNCTION, and LLANGYNOG.—Great Western (late Cambrian).

Miles	Down.	Week Days only. mrn	mrn A	aft B	aft A	aft W	aft S	....
—	**Oswestry** ....dep.	8 0	1135	1 55	4 20	4 50	5 30	....
4½	Porthywaen...............	8 12	1148	2 8	4 33	5 3	5 43	....
6	Blodwell Junction.. arr.	8 15	1151	2 11	4 37	5 7	5 47	....
	dep.	8 16	1152	2 12	4 38	5 8	5 48	....
6¾	Llanyblodwell............	8 20	1158	2 18	4 44	5 14	5 54	....
7¾	Glanyrafon	z	z	z	z	z	z	
9¼	Llansilin Road...........	8 30	12 8	2 28	4 54	5 25	6 4	....
10¼	Llangedwyn..............	8 35	1213	2 33	5 0	5 32	6 11	....
12¾	Pentrefelin..............	8 42	1222	2 42	5 7	5 40	6 19	....
14	Llanrhaiadr Mochnant §..	8 48	1229	2 47	5 13	5 45	6 24	....
15½	Pedair Ffordd ‖	8 54	1235	2 53	5 18	5 55	6 30	....
16¾	Penybontfawr............	9 2	1243	3 1	5 26	6 3	6 38	....
19½	**Llangynog** ....arr.	9 12	1253	3 11	5 36	6 13	6 48	....

Miles	Up.	Week Days only. mrn W	mrn	aft B	aft A	aft A	aft W	aft S
—	**Llangynog** ....dep.	7 0	9 35	1 0	1 30	5 55	6 30	7 0
2¾	Penybontfawr............	7 8	9 43	1 9	1 38	6 3	6 38	7 8
4¼	Pedair Ffordd ‖	7 20	9 50	1 16	1 45	6 10	6 45	7 15
5½	Llanrhaiadr Mochnant §..	7 25	9 55	1 21	1 55	6 15	6 50	7 20
6¾	Pentrefelin..............	7 35	10 0	1 26	2 0	6 20	6 55	7 25
8¾	Llangedwyn..............	7 41	10 5	1 31	2 6	6 25	7 0	7 30
10¼	Llansilin Road...........	7 52	1012	1 37	2 13	6 32	7 7	7 37
11¾	Glanyrafon	z	z	z	z	z	z	z
12¾	Llanyblodwell............	8 5	1019	1 46	2 2[illegible]	6 40	7 15	7 45
13½	Blodwell Junction.. arr.	8 9	1023	1 48	2 23	6 42	7 17	7 47
	dep.	8 10	1024	1 49	2 24	6 43	7 18	7 48
15	Porthywaen...............	8 21	1028	1 54	2 30	6 50	7 25	7 55
19½	**Oswestry 136, 138** ..arr.	8 40	1045	2 10	2 45	7 5	7 40	8 10

A Except Wednesdays and Saturdays.
B Wednesdays and Saturdays.
S Saturdays only.
W Wednesdays only.
z Stop when required.
§ Station 1½ miles from Llanrhaiadr Mochnant.
‖ Station 1¼ miles from Llanrhaiadr Mochnant.

July 1924

OSWESTRY, BLODWELL JUNCTION, and LLANGYNOG

Miles		Week Days only a.m Wednesdays only	a.m Except Wednesdays		p.m Except Saturdays	p.m Saturdays only			
—	**Oswestry**.. .... dep	7 15	7 35	..	4 30	5 25	..	..	..
4½	**Porthywaen**............	7 27	7 47	..	4 42	5 37	..	..	..
6	**Blodwell Junction**......	7 34	7 55	..	4 50	5 45	..	..	..
6¾	**Llanyblodwell**	7 39	7 59	..	4 54	5 50	..	..	..
8	**Glanyrafon**...............	7 44	8 4	..	4 59	5 55	..	..	..
9½	**Llansilin Road**...........	7 49	8 9	..	5 4	6 0	..	..	..
10¾	**Llangedwyn**............	7 54	8 14	.	5 10	6 5	..	..	..
12¾	**Pentrefelin**	8 1	8 20	..	5 15	6 12	..	..	..
14½	**Llanrhaiadr Mochnant**..	8 7	8 26	..	5 22	6 20	..	..	..
15½	**Pedair Ffordd**	8 13	8 32	..	5 27	6 25	..	..	..
17	**Penybontfawr**..........	8 20	8 37	..	5 32	6 32	..	..	..
19½	**Llangynog** .... arr	8 32	8 50	..	5 43	6 44	..	..	..

Miles		Week Days only a.m Wednesdays only	a.m Except Wednesdays		p.m Except Saturdays	p.m Saturdays only				
—	**Llangynog** .... dep	8 40	9 0	..	5 53	6 55	..	..	..	..
2¾	**Penybontfawr**..........	8 54	9 11	..	6 5	7 6	..	..	..	..
4¼	**Pedair Ffordd**	9 0	9 18	..	6 11	7 13	..	..	..	..
5½	Llanrhaiadr Mochnant	9 12	9 22	..	6 15	7 17	..	..	..	..
6¾	**Pentrefelin**	9 17	9 28	..	6 21	7 23	..	..	..	..
8¾	Llangedwyn	9 25	9 35	..	6 29	7 30	..	..	..	..
10¼	LlansilinRoad..........	9 35	9 40	..	6 34	7 35	..	..	..	..
11½	Glanyrafon	9 40	9 45	..	6 38	7 40	..	..	..	..
12¾	Llanyblodwell	9 45	9 50	..	6 43	7 45	..	..	..	..
13½	Blodwell Junction......	9 49	9 54	..	6 47	7 49	..	..	..	..
14¾	Porthywaen	9 55	10 0	..	6 53	7 57	..	..	..	..
19½	Oswestry .... arr	1013	1013	..	7 6	8 10	..	..	..	..

June 1950

CAMBRIAN, SHREWSBURY and WELSHPOOL

Down. For arrivals at *Whitchurch, p. 126.*	Week Days. 1,2,3 mix	1,2,3 mrn		1,2,3 mix	1,2,3 mrn	1,2,3 aft	1&2 aft	1,2,3 aft	1,2,3 aft	1,2,3 aft	1,2,3 aft	Sndys 1,2,3 mrn	1,2,3 aft
Crewe 126 dep	....	....		....	8 35	....	1230	....	....	5 15	8 35	....	....
Whitchurch ..dep	1&2 class mail on Shrewsbury and Welshpool Line. ☞	....		7 50	9 30	....	1 12	....	....	6 30	9 18	....	....
Fenn's Bank......		....		7 55	b	....	....	....	....	6 38	9 25	....	....
Bettisfield		....		8 3	b	....	d	....	....	6 45	9 33	....	....
Welshampton		....		8 8	b	....	d	....	....	6 50	9 37	....	....
Ellesmere		....		8 23	9 56	....	1 32	....	....	6 57	9 44	....	....
Frankton		....		8 33	b	....	....	....	....	....	....	....	....
Whittington **19, 20**		....		8 48	1015	....	1 47	....	....	7 10	9 50	....	....
Oswestry .. arr		....		9 0	1020	....	1 50	....	....	7 15	10 0	....	....
G.W.L., 19, 20 dep		6 10		Stop	1030	i	2 5	3 20	4 15	7 25	Stop	6 15	....
Llynclys.........		6 20			1037	....	2 18	3 28	4 25	7 34		6 25	....
Pant		....			....	....	....	3 32	4 30	....	....	....	....
Llanymynech **129**		6 25			1045	....	2 20	3 36	4 35	7 40	....	6 31	....
Four Crosses......		6 31			1052	....	b	3 42	Stop	7 45	....	6 35	....
Arddleen		....			g	....	....	3 47		....	....	....	....
Pool Quay		6 41		Except Mondays and Thurs. Machynlleth and Aber	11 2	....	f	3 52	Mondays only. ☞	7 55	....	6 44	....
Buttington........		6 47			11 8	....	2 35	3 57		8 1	1&2	6 50	....
Welshpool 1 ..arr		6 53			1115	....	2 40	4 5		8 8	aft	6 55	....
Shrewsbury & Welshpool. Shrewsbury d	3 30	6 0			1030	....	1 45	Stop		5 45	8 10	6 0	4 45
Hanwood	....	6 12			e	....	b			5 58	8 30	6 15	4 58
Yockleton....	....	6 22			1050	....	b			6 8	....	6 25	5 6
Westbury	....	6 32			11 0	....	2 12			6 18	9 15	6 35	5 18
Middletown ..	....	6 42			1110	....	....	—		6 28	....	6 45	5 25
Buttington ..	....	6 48			1117	....	2 30		1,2,3	6 35	9 30	6 55	5 38
Welshpool 1 a	4 35	6 55			1122	....	2 35		aft	6 40	9 40	7 0	5 40
Welshpool ....dep	4 40	7 0	8 45		1125	....	2 50		4 50	8 16	—	7 5	Stop
Forden	....	7 2	9 5		b	....	....		5 0	b	—	7 17	
Montgomery	5 0	7 18	9 16		1142	....	3 5		5 5	8 33		7 25	....
Abermule 129....	....	7 28	9 36		1151	....	....		5 15	8 43		7 35	....
Newtown	5 22	7 40	10 4		12 1	....	3 25		5 25	8 53		7 48	....

b Stop when required on informing the Guard.

June 1869

LLANFYLLIN BRANCH.—Cambrian.

All 1,2,3 cl.	mrn	mrn	a	aft	aft	Up.	mrn	mrn	aft	a	aft
Llanymynech	7 50	1145	2 25	4 40	7 45	Llanfyllin dep	5 50	10 0	1 45	3 5	6 25
Llansaintffraid	8 5	12 0	2 40	4 55	8 0	Llanfechain ..	6 4	1014	1 59	3 19	6 39
Llanfechain ..	8 11	12 6	2 46	5 1	8 6	Llansaintffraid	6 10	1020	2 5	3 25	6 45
Llanfyllin arr	8 25	1220	3 0	5 15	8 20	Llanymynech.	6 25	1035	2 20	3 40	7 0

a Thursdays only. ☞ The Trains stop at Brongwyn when required.

June 1869

LLANYMYNECH and LLANFYLLIN

Mls		Week Days only a.m	a.m		p.m	p.m		p.m Except Saturdays	p.m Sats. only	
—	Llanymynech ...... dep	8 33	1113	..	3 59	6 35	..	8 25	9 25	..
¾	Carreghofa Halt........	8 36	1116	..	4 2	6 38	..	8 28	9 28	..
3¼	Llansantffraid..........	8 42	1122	..	4 8	6 44	..	8 34	9 34	..
5	Llanfechain.............	8 47	1127	..	4 13	6 48	..	8 39	9 39	..
6½	Bryngwyn	8 52	1132	..	4 19	6 54	..	8 45	9 46	..
8½	Llanfyllin........... arr	8 57	1138	..	4 24	6 59	..	8 50	9 51	..

Mls		Week Days only a.m	a.m		p.m Sats. only	p.m Except Saturdays	p.m		p.m Sats. only	p.m Except Saturdays	
—	Llanfyllin.......... dep	7 18	1015	..	1 10	1 25	4 35	..	7 15	7 50	..
1¾	Bryngwyn	7 23	1020	—	1 15	1 30	4 40	..	7 20	7 55	..
3½	Llanfechain.............	7 28	1025	..	1 20	1 35	4 45	..	7 25	8 0	..
5¼	Llansantffraid	7 33	1030	..	1 25	1 40	4 50	..	7 30	8 5	..
7¾	Carreghofa Halt.........	7 39	1036	..	1 31	1 46	4 56	..	7 36	8 11	..
8½	Llanymynech...... arr	7 42	1039	..	1 34	1 49	4 59	..	7 39	8 14	..

June 1950

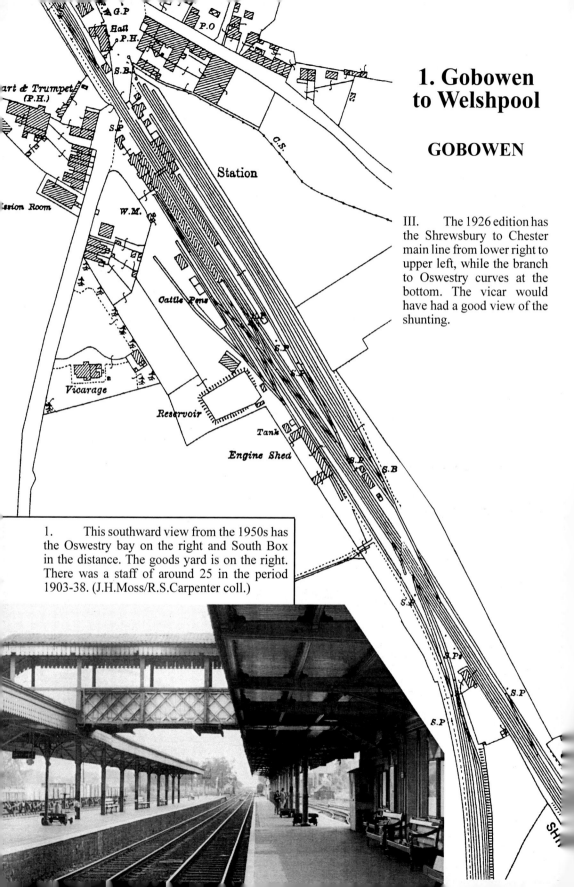

1. Gobowen to Welshpool

GOBOWEN

III. The 1926 edition has the Shrewsbury to Chester main line from lower right to upper left, while the branch to Oswestry curves at the bottom. The vicar would have had a good view of the shunting.

Station

Cattle Pens

Vicarage

Reservoir

Tank

Engine Shed

W.M.

1. This southward view from the 1950s has the Oswestry bay on the right and South Box in the distance. The goods yard is on the right. There was a staff of around 25 in the period 1903-38. (J.H.Moss/R.S.Carpenter coll.)

2.	The extent of the goods yard was recorded from a departing up train, some time before its closure on 2nd November 1964. It reopened as a coal concentration depot on 6th December 1971. (A.Dudman coll.)

3.	A train from Oswestry arrives behind 0-6-0PT no. 5422 and behind it is the branch line, which can be seen to be independent of the main line. (A.J.B.Dodd/P.Chancellor coll.)

4.   It is 29th July 1963 and 2-6-2T no. 41285 is departing, propelling its two coaches to Oswestry. Part of South Box is above the leading coach. (M.Hale)

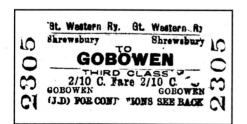

5.   The buildings were completed in 1846 and recently listed Grade II. A £0.3m restoration scheme ended in April 1989 and the down side is seen on 26th June 2008 from the 10.17 Marylebone to Wrexham, then part of a freshly restored London service. (V.Mitchell)

6.   The up side canopy and buildings of about 1900 were recorded on the same day and the still-functional signal box is in the distance. The former crossing cottage was adapted as a booking office and was operated by pupils of Moreton Hall School from 7th July 1993. (V.Mitchell)

PARK HALL HALT

7.   The halt opened on 5th July 1926 and its location is indicated on map II. It is 1949 and a northbound train approaches the platform and Gobowen's distant signal. The area had housed German prisoners during World War I. (SLS coll.)

8.   A class 101 DMU calls on 30th August 1966 on its way from Gobowen to Oswestry. The nearby hospital was the main purpose of the halt. (H.Ballantyne)

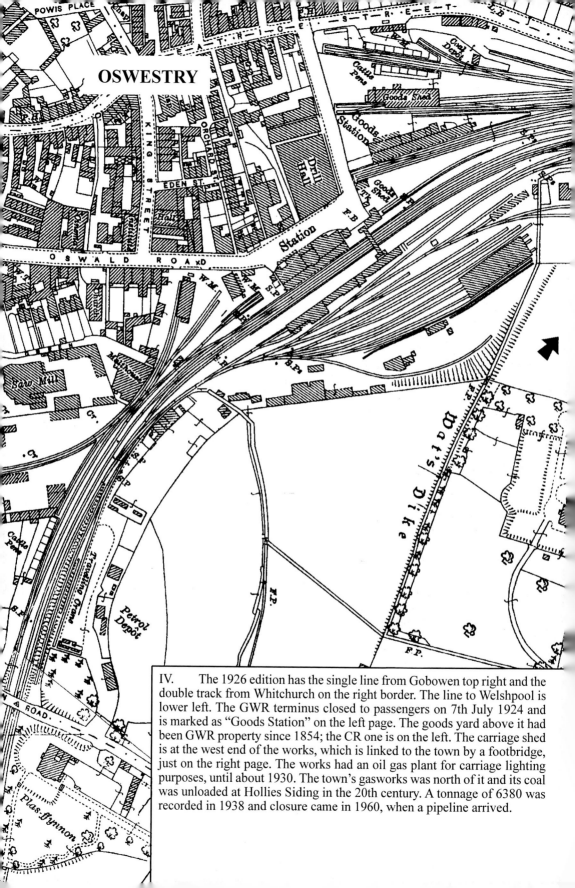

OSWESTRY

IV. The 1926 edition has the single line from Gobowen top right and the double track from Whitchurch on the right border. The line to Welshpool is lower left. The GWR terminus closed to passengers on 7th July 1924 and is marked as "Goods Station" on the left page. The goods yard above it had been GWR property since 1854; the CR one is on the left. The carriage shed is at the west end of the works, which is linked to the town by a footbridge, just on the right page. The works had an oil gas plant for carriage lighting purposes, until about 1930. The town's gasworks was north of it and its coal was unloaded at Hollies Siding in the 20th century. A tonnage of 6380 was recorded in 1938 and closure came in 1960, when a pipeline arrived.

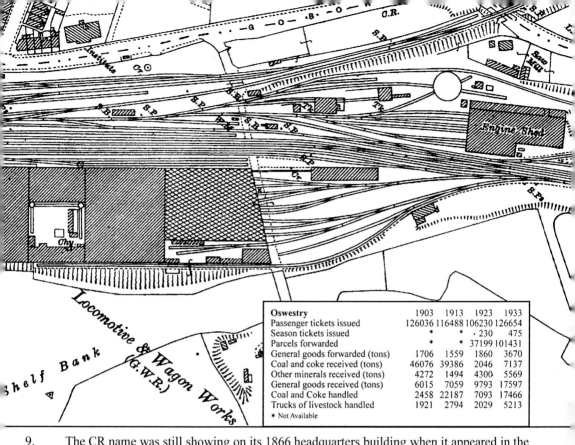

Oswestry	1903	1913	1923	1933
Passenger tickets issued	126036	116488	106230	126654
Season tickets issued	*	*	230	475
Parcels forwarded	*	*	37199	101431
General goods forwarded (tons)	1706	1559	1860	3670
Coal and coke received (tons)	46076	39386	2046	7137
Other minerals received (tons)	4272	1494	4300	5569
General goods received (tons)	6015	7059	9793	17597
Coal and Coke handled	2458	22187	7093	17466
Trucks of livestock handled	1921	2794	2029	5213

* Not Available

9.   The CR name was still showing on its 1866 headquarters building when it appeared in the GWR Magazine upon the takeover in 1922. The term "General Offices" was used. (GWR)

10.   The CR established its works here in 1866 and locomotives were repaired here for a century, carriages and wagons for a little less. Seen in 1926 are mostly 0-6-0 locos, but the one with a round window (centre) is a Nasmyth Wilson 0-4-4T, ex-CR. (GWR)

11.   This was the largest engine shed on the CR and it is on the right of the map. Posing on 28th August 1926 is the crew of "Duke of Cornwall" class 4-4-0 no. 3280 *Tregenna*. (H.C.Casserley)

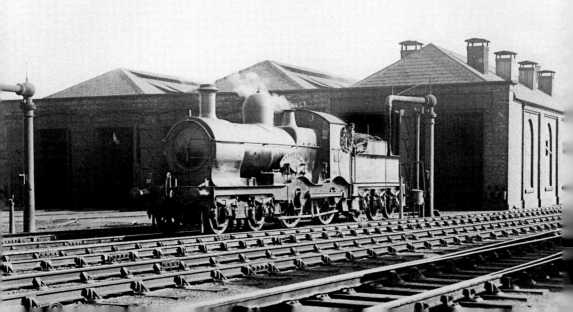

12.　　Shunting on the same day is 0-4-2T no. 574 one of the 517 class. The GWR goods shed is in the background; the staff was 23 in 1903 and 28 in 1913 for both goods and passenger work. (H.C.Casserley)

13.　　We are looking west from a point near the centre of the right page of the map. A Tanat Valley train is waiting on the short siding north of the works, while the long footbridge is in the distance on 6th August 1935. Centre is North Box which dated from about 1924. Its 96-lever frame was in use until 8th November 1970. There were two earlier boxes behind the camera and both are shown on the map. (H.F.Wheeller/R.S.Carpenter coll.)

14. Typical GWR architecture was to be found for its terminal building, which was photographed in the 1930s. The initial temporary station lasted until 1866 and this one was completed in about 1885. There was a similar design at Ross-on-Wye, now recreated at Kidderminster by the Severn Valley Railway. (Unknown)

15. The total staff numbered 131 in 1923, but this was down to 101 by 1934. A Tanat Valley train is about to be shunted on 13th March 1948 by 0-4-2T no. 1197. It was ex-CR no. 59 *Seaham*, built by Sharp Stewart in 1866. (W.A.Camwell/SLS coll.)

16.   The GWR shed coding was OSW and BR used 89A until December 1960, 89D from January 1961 and 6E from September 1963. Closure came on 18th January 1965. There were 36 locomotives based here at the end of 1947. The photograph is from 26th January 1950. (R.S.Carpenter)

17.   A view northwest on 20th September 1958 gives a good impression of the extent of the offices. The 2-6-0 is no. 46509 and it appears again in branch pictures. South Box (left) had been completed in 1892 and had 42 levers when closed on 8th November 1970. (H.C.Casserley)

18.   The 2.5pm Welshpool to Whitchurch on 24th October 1964 was hauled by no. 80104, a class 4 2-6-4T of the type built at Brighton from 1951 onwards. Parcels traffic was moved to Gobowen from about 1966 to 1971. This is South box. (E.Wilmshurst)

19.   Goods traffic continued until 6th December 1971 and this panorama is from 5th August 1972. The diverging platforms carried the ex-GWR building, while the remaining CR one is on the curved former up platform. There had been a 6-ton crane on the GWR site, which had two signal boxes from 1895 to 1924, with 27 and 9 levers respectively. The bay in the centre was added in 1924, when the GWR station closed. (A.M.Davies)

20. The Cambrian Railways Society took a lease on the CR goods yard part of the site in 1972, but stone traffic continued between Gobowen and Blodwell Junction until 1989. The CRS formed a trust which set about restoring part of the route between Llynclys South and Pant. Peckett 0-4-0ST no. 2131 of 1951 was in action with an autocoach on 11th July 1982, but passenger traffic was a long way off. (T.Heavyside)

21. Seen on 8th June 2002 is no. 7822 *Foxcote Manor*, which was visiting the CRS from its base on the Llangollen Railway. South box and the main building are evident; a new level crossing had been created under the photographer's feet. Prospects have improved subsequently for a lengthy journey, both north and south. The excellent CRS Museum is open most days. (T.Heavyside)

WESTON WHARF

V.   The 1926 edition includes a long loading dock. The goods shed was provided with a 15-cwt crane.

22.   The former CR Works was photographed from the long footbridge in October 2004. The track had not carried a train for 15 years, but privately owned stock was accumulating. The Gobowen line had been on the land in front of the locomotives. All the stock had gone by 2009 and the premises were the subject of major alterations for new uses. (P.O'Callaghan)

23a.   Weston Wharf goods depot was almost two miles from Oswestry and was in use for public goods traffic until 5th June 1961. It was subsequently used for potato storage and then for car body repairs until purchased by the CRS. A recent acquisition stands at the bottom of a temporary ramp in August 2009. (E.Jones)

23b.   In its early life, the shed had been used for grain and products of the nearby mill. This photograph from 2nd September 2009 shows rolling stock from the local waterworks on a demonstration track. (L.Wass)

LLYNCLYS
JUNCTION

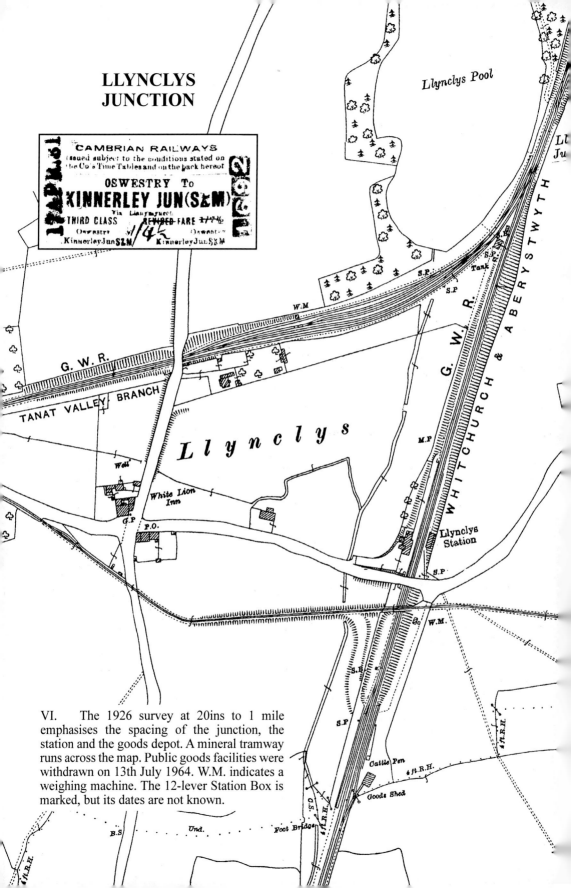

Llynclys Pool

CAMBRIAN RAILWAYS
issued subject to the conditions stated on
the Co's Time Tables and on the back hereof

OSWESTRY To
KINNERLEY JUN (S&M)
Via Llanymynech
THIRD CLASS   REVISED FARE 1/7½
Oswestry   1/4½   Oswestry
Kinnerley Jun S&M   Kinnerley Jun S&M

Llynclys Pool

G. W. R.

TANAT VALLEY BRANCH

L l y n c l y s

W.M.

S.P.

Tank

S.P.

Well

White Lion
Inn

G.P.

P.O.

Llynclys
Station

M.P.

S.P.

W.M.

S.B.

Cattle Pen

4 ft. R.H.

S.P.

G.S.

Goods Shed

Foot Bridge

B.S.   Und.

G. W. R.

WHITCHURCH & ABERYSTWYTH

VI.   The 1926 survey at 20ins to 1 mile
emphasises the spacing of the junction, the
station and the goods depot. A mineral tramway
runs across the map. Public goods facilities were
withdrawn on 13th July 1964. W.M. indicates a
weighing machine. The 12-lever Station Box is
marked, but its dates are not known.

24.   Seen between the signals in 1904 is a coal stage used by engines shunting the branch to Nantmawr, Blodwell and Porthywaen Quarries. The water column was supplied from the tank on the left. (R.S.Carpenter coll.)

25.　A southward view in November 1964 features the junction signals. The sidings on the left are top right on the map. The box had a 31-lever frame and was in use from 5th September 1892 to 14th May 1967. (A.M.Davies)

26.　This is the signalman's view of the Tanat Valley branch on 8th October 1966. The end of steam was imminent. (A.Moyes/A.M.Davies coll.)

LLYNCLYS

27.　　Seen in 1904, the station had a staff of 11 when first under GWR control in 1923. From 1929 to 1938, eight men were listed. The building was in residential use in 2009, but painted white. (R.S.Carpenter coll.)

Llynclys	1923	1929	1930	1933
Passenger tickets issued	8808	5410	4455	4149
Season tickets issued	34	30	24	20
Parcels forwarded	9475	7067	7913	709
General goods forwarded (tons)	109	67	54	23
Coal and coke received (tons)	1327	982	945	29
Other minerals received (tons)	1478	1016	692	1173
General goods received (tons)	2861	189	169	80
Coal and Coke handled	6697	7691	5377	598
Trucks of livestock handled	13	30	19	3

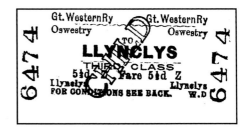

28.   A northward panorama from the road bridge has the junction box and water tank in the distance. At the end of the up platform is the lamp hut and a water column. Part of the track in the distance was relaid in 2003. (W.A.Camwell/SLS coll.)

29.   The junction is in the background as 4-4-0 no. 9084 *Isle of Jersey* rumbles through on 6th April 1951. One of the "Duke of Cornwall" class built in 1899, it carried this number from 1946 until withdrawn in 1951. (M.J.Stretton coll.)

30.   An Ivatt 2-6-0 arrives from Welshpool, sometime in the 1950s. Beyond the bridge is an abutment which once supported a bridge for the tramway, while in the distance is the roof of the goods shed. This area was occupied by the Cambrian Railways Trust and ¾ mile of track had been relaid by 2009, with the aim of joining it to the Gobowen-Blodwell Junction mineral line, which had been idle since 1989. A class 101 DMU and a class 08 diesel locomotive were on site. The Trust and the Society would be united again. (R.S.Carpenter)

Track diagram in August 2009 created from
    a satellite image from Google Earth.

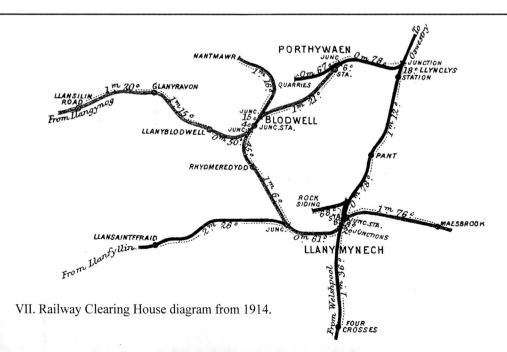

VII. Railway Clearing House diagram from 1914.

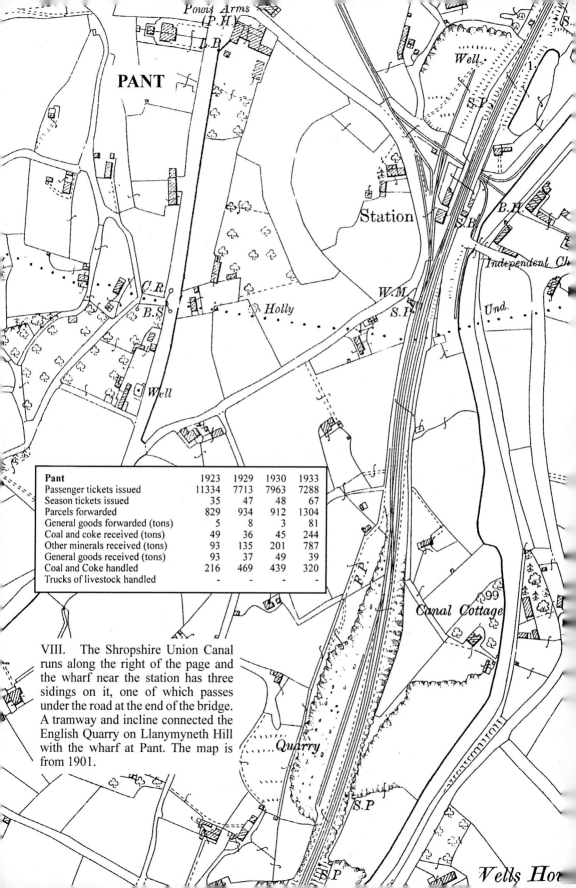

PANT

Powis Arms
(P.H.)
L.B.

Well

Station

B.H.

S.B.

Independent Ch.

C.R.

B.S.

Holly

W.M.
S.P.

Und.

Well

Pant	1923	1929	1930	1933
Passenger tickets issued	11334	7713	7963	7288
Season tickets issued	35	47	48	67
Parcels forwarded	829	934	912	1304
General goods forwarded (tons)	5	8	3	81
Coal and coke received (tons)	49	36	45	244
Other minerals received (tons)	93	135	201	787
General goods received (tons)	93	37	49	39
Coal and Coke handled	216	469	439	320
Trucks of livestock handled	-	-	-	-

Canal Cottage

99

VIII. The Shropshire Union Canal
runs along the right of the page and
the wharf near the station has three
sidings on it, one of which passes
under the road at the end of the bridge.
A tramway and incline connected the
English Quarry on Llanymyneth Hill
with the wharf at Pant. The map is
from 1901.

Quarry

S.P.

Vells Hoi

31. The station was listed as having two men in the period 1923-38. This southward view from August 1964 was taken from above the tunnel under the platform, which had earlier carried the quarry line to the canal wharf. (H.C.Casserley)

32. The canal bridge is on the right as no. 7819 *Hinton Manor* accelerates south on 28th November 1964. It is preserved on the Severn Valley Railway. Lower quadrant signals persisted to the end. The route between Oswestry and Llanymynech was doubled in 1900. The goods yard had been on the left, but it had closed way back on 22nd March 1915. The box had 16 levers, which were used between about 1893 and 1965. (A.M.Davies)

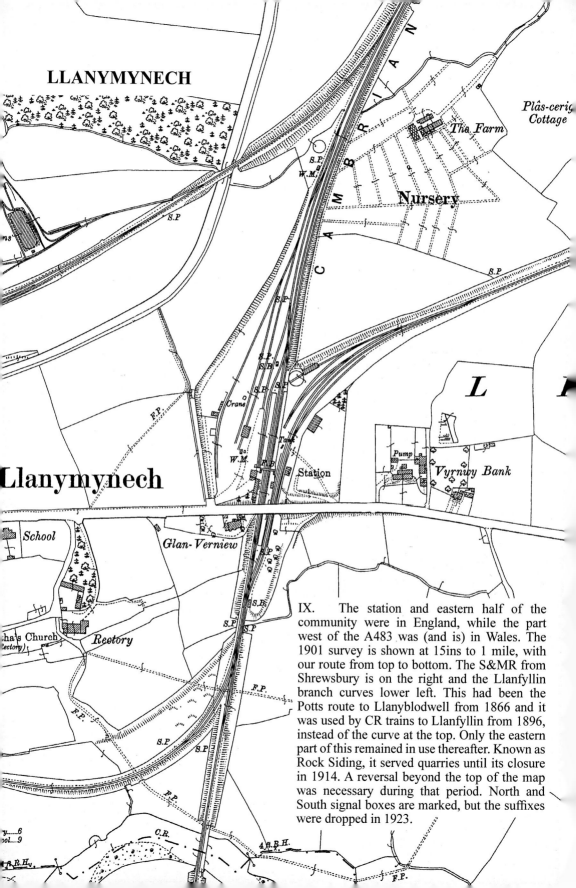

LLANYMYNECH

Plâs-ceriç
Cottage

The Farm

Nursery

S.P.
S.P.
W.M.

S.P.

S.P.

S.P.
S/B

S.P. S.P.

Crane

L

Pump

Vyrnwy Bank

Tank
W.M.

Station

Llanymynech

Glan-Verniew

School

S.P.

S.P.

F.P.

S.P.
S.B.

a's Church
Rectory)
Rectory

S.P.
S.P.

F.P.

F.P.

S.P.

S.P.

F.P.

y....6
ool..9

C.R.

4 ft R.H.

A.R.H.

F.P.

IX.   The station and eastern half of the
community were in England, while the part
west of the A483 was (and is) in Wales. The
1901 survey is shown at 15ins to 1 mile, with
our route from top to bottom. The S&MR from
Shrewsbury is on the right and the Llanfyllin
branch curves lower left. This had been the
Potts route to Llanyblodwell from 1866 and it
was used by CR trains to Llanfyllin from 1896,
instead of the curve at the top. Only the eastern
part of this remained in use thereafter. Known as
Rock Siding, it served quarries until its closure
in 1914. A reversal beyond the top of the map
was necessary during that period. North and
South signal boxes are marked, but the suffixes
were dropped in 1923.

33.   CR no. 15 *Glansevern* is standing with a Blodwell Junction train. These travelled along the Llanfyllin branch for about one mile, before turning north. This connection closed in 1925. The locomotive was built by Sharp Stewart in 1875 and withdrawn in 1908. This rare photograph was taken in about 1904. (R.S.Carpenter coll.)

34.   No. 5816 pauses with an Oswestry-Llanfyllin service on 5th August 1935. Modern GWR coaches contrast with the antiquated S&MR stock. There was a staff of 9 or 10 in the 1930s. (H.F.Wheeller/R.S.Carpenter coll.)

35.   The 10.50am Oswestry to Aberystwyth is arriving on 26th August 1946, while ex-LNER class J69 0-6-0T no. 7388 serves as War Department no. 70084. Note the limestone quarry face in the background. (W.A.Camwell/SLS coll.)

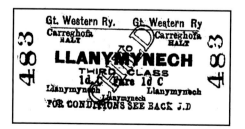

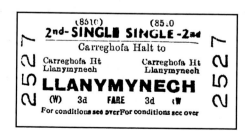

36.   A northward panorama features contrasting architecture and much of the goods yard. Included is the cattle dock, but not the crane, which was rated at 3 tons 5 cwt. (W.A.Camwell/SLS coll.)

37.   A third picture on the same day features GWR 0-4-2T no. 4812 with the 11.13am Llanymynech to Llanfyllin branch train. WD no. 70084 is seen again. The loading gauges mark the boundary between the GWR and the S&MR. (W.A.Camwell/SLS coll.)

38.   An ex-LNWR 0-6-0 appears to be propelling an S&MR train towards the platforms and it seems to include the four-wheeled former royal saloon. Trains were run for civilian workers until 1960. (J.Langford coll.)

→ 39. The last train on the S&MR was this special run by the SLS and formed of two coaches, plus a brake van, hauled by WD Hunslet 0-6-0ST no. 193. It is about to depart for Kinnerley on 20th March 1960. (D.A.Johnson)

→ 40. The GWR provided a staff of 9 or 10 for its part of the station in the 1930s. The up side buildings were recorded in their entirety on 18th May 1963. (P.Kingston)

For other views of this station and a journey on the S&MR, please see our *Branch Line to Shrewsbury*.

41.　On the same day, 2-6-0 no. 46512 runs in with a Llanfyllin to Oswestry train. Goods yard closure took place on 6th July 1964. In the distance is the 47-lever signal box. There was a 20-lever one at the north end, but it was not a block post. (P.Kingston)

42.　The afternoon school train was photographed sometime in 1964, working towards Oswestry. The 0-4-2T is carrying the "Lion & Monocycle" emblem of BR. (P.Ward/SLS coll.)

t Farm

House

Domgay Chapel
(Congl.)

Domgay Cottage

t Cottage

Hafod-Offa

FOUR CROSSES

S.P

S.P

S.P

sses

The Clawdd

F.P.

Station

S.B

W.M.

Pump

Crane

Greenfield House

Railway
Terrace

City House

The Grove

F.P.

Manse

P

P

X.   Close examination of the
earthworks in the centre of this
1901 map will show that it is not of
railway origin, but part of Offas's
Dyke which separated Wales and
England. The Four Crosses public
house is at the road junction on the
left. The full length of the passing
loop is included.

F.P.

RIAN

RAILWAY

Hampto

F.P.

43.   The down waiting room is featured in this view from the goods yard. This contained a 6-ton crane for much of its life. There were five employees for most of the 1930s. The creamery is in the background. (P.Ward/SLS coll.)

➜   44. Looking south in August 1961, we can admire the choice of barge boards and part of the well kept garden. The tablet catcher is on the left, with netting below it. (R.G.Nelson/T.Walsh coll.)

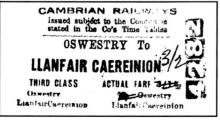

CAMBRIAN RAILWAYS
Issued subject to the Conditions
stated in the Co's Time Tables
OSWESTRY To
LLANFAIR CAEREINION 3/2
THIRD CLASS   ACTUAL FARE 3/1½
Oswestry   Oswestry
LlanfairCaereinion   Llanfair Caereinion

➜   45. A northward panorama in November 1964 includes part of the goods yard, which closed that month. The 1925 signal box had 26 levers. (A.M.Davies)

ARDDLEEN HALT

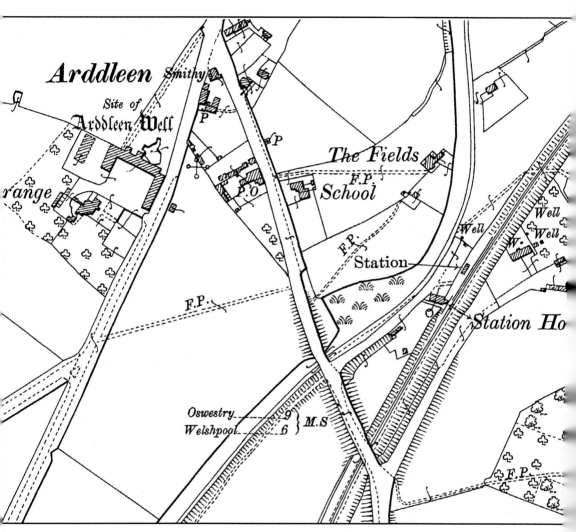

XI.   The 1902 edition has the Shropshire Union Canal curving across it, with the station entrance on the lane parallel to the towpath. The name first appeared in timetables in February 1862.

46.   The station house was unusual in not being parallel to the railway, suggesting that it predated the line. It has no railway architectural features. In the early years, trains called only on certain days. (P.Ward/SLS coll.)

47.   The 27½ milepost is common to both photographs. This one is from 21st July 1963. The term HALT was added in 1954. (P.J.Garland/R.S.Carpenter coll.)

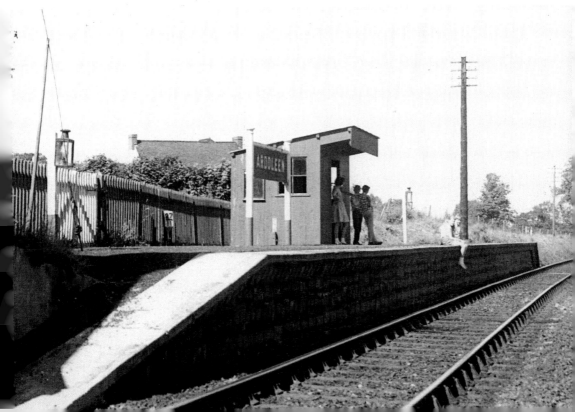

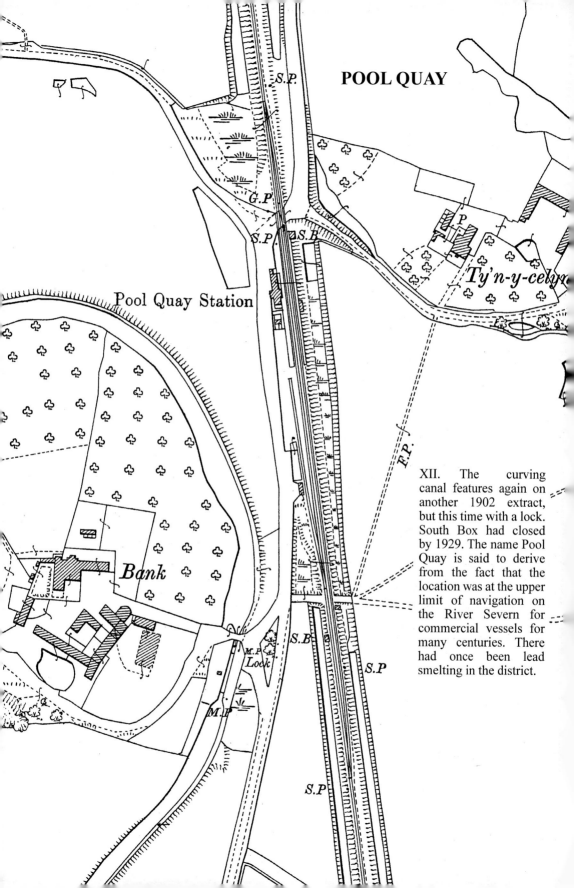

POOL QUAY

S.P.

G.P.

S.P. S.B

Pool Quay Station

Ty'n-y-celyn

P
P

F.P.

Bank

S.B

M.P.
Lock

M.P.

S.P

S.P

XII. The curving canal features again on another 1902 extract, but this time with a lock. South Box had closed by 1929. The name Pool Quay is said to derive from the fact that the location was at the upper limit of navigation on the River Severn for commercial vessels for many centuries. There had once been lead smelting in the district.

48. The end of the single siding is just included in this northward view. The staffing level was five in the 1930s. The white posts were for single line equipment. (P.Ward/SLS coll.)

49. We can now enjoy three photographs from 25th September 1959. No. 7810 *Draycott Manor* is accelerating south with a glandular problem and two coaches for Welshpool. (R.G.Nelson/T.Walsh)

50.   The A483 was in close proximity to the station and crossed the line here. Its alignment is now to the left of the picture. (R.G.Nelson/T.Walsh)

51.   The second platform (left) was added in 1898 (in timber) with the completion of the passing loop. In the distance is the goods yard which closed on 4th May 1964. (R.G.Nelson/T.Walsh)

52.　　The tablet pouches are being exchanged on 2nd June 1962 as no. 7809 *Childrey Manor* passes with the 8.20am Oswestry to Aberystwyth, all stations from Llanymynech. (A.M.Davies)

53.　　The signal box is fitted with a gate wheel, so necessary on this busy road. Traffic waits for an up train on 28th August 1964. The 1896 box had twenty levers. (H.C.Casserley)

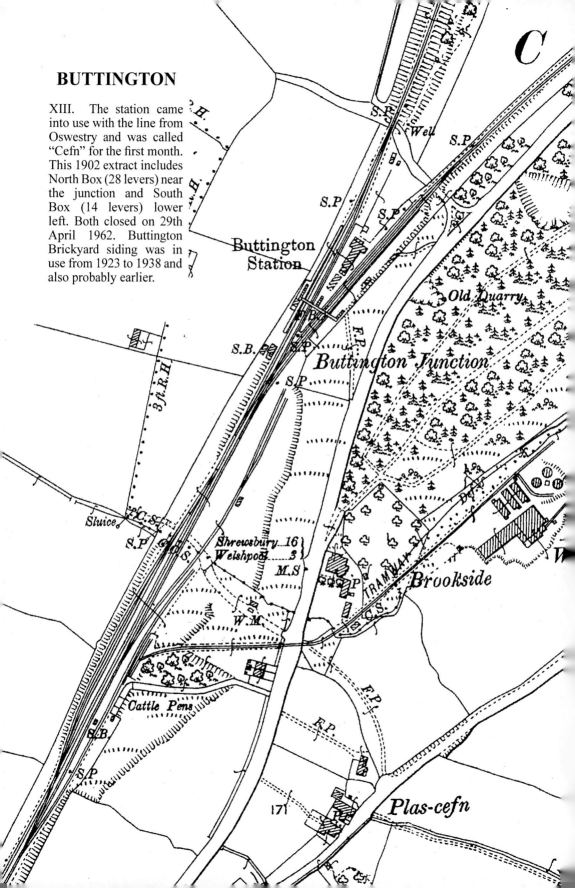

BUTTINGTON

XIII. The station came into use with the line from Oswestry and was called "Cefn" for the first month. This 1902 extract includes North Box (28 levers) near the junction and South Box (14 levers) lower left. Both closed on 29th April 1962. Buttington Brickyard siding was in use from 1923 to 1938 and also probably earlier.

C

Well

S.P.

S.P.

S.P.

S.P.

Buttington Station

Old Quarry

S.B.

S.P.

Buttington Junction

S.P.

3 ft. R.H.

3 ft. R.H.

Sluice

C.S.

S.P.

C.S.

Shrewsbury 16

Welshpool 3

M.S.

TRAMWAY

C.S.

Brookside

W.M.

Cattle Pens

S.B.

S.P.

171

Plas-cefn

54.   A panorama from the footbridge in the mid-1930s has the LMS/GWR joint line to Shrewsbury on the right and the convergence of the Oswestry tracks on the left. (Stations UK)

55.   There was a staff of nine throughout the 1930s. This view is from the early 1950s; the end of that decade saw the loss of the footbridge and the shortening of the platform on the left. (J.H.Moss/R.S.Carpenter coll.)

56.   Ex-GWR 4-4-0 no. 9017 stands with an Oswestry to Welshpool train on 29th February 1952. The 9000 "Dukedog" class was introduced in 1936. (P.Q.Treloar coll.)

57.   The two exchange sidings and the junction are in the distance on 25th September 1959. Part of the up platform was built of timber, owing to the instability of the ground. The route to Welshpool comprised two single tracks until 1893. (R.G.Nelson/T.Walsh)

58.   No. 46513 was recorded on the same day running from Oswestry to Welshpool. The station and the small goods yard both closed on 12th September 1960, five years ahead of the Oswestry route. No trace now remains. (R.G.Nelson/T.Walsh)

CAMBRIAN RAILWAYS
Issued subject to the Conditions
stated in the Co's Time Tables
LLANGEDWYN To
WELSHPOOL
THIRD CLASS   P'VISED FARE 2/6
Llangedwyn   Llangedwyn
Welshpool   Welshpool

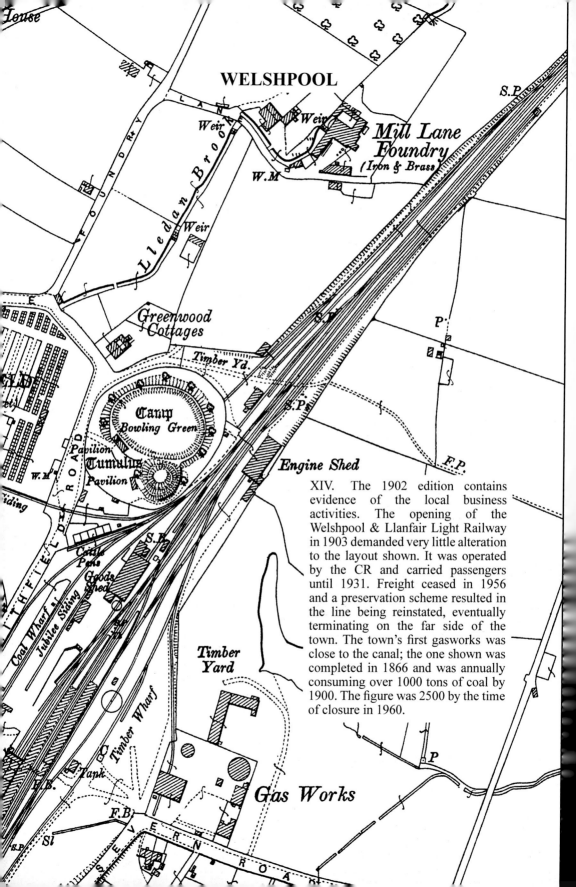

WELSHPOOL

Weir

Weir

Mill Lane Foundry
(Iron & Brass)

W.M

Weir

S.P

Llcdan Brook

Foundry Lane

Greenwood Cottages

P

Timber Yd.

O.P

S.P

Camp
Bowling Green

Pavilion

Tumulus

Pavilion

W.M

ROAD

Engine Shed

F.P

Siding

...iding

SMITHFIELD ROAD

S.P

Cattle Pens

Goods Shed

XIV. The 1902 edition contains evidence of the local business activities. The opening of the Welshpool & Llanfair Light Railway in 1903 demanded very little alteration to the layout shown. It was operated by the CR and carried passengers until 1931. Freight ceased in 1956 and a preservation scheme resulted in the line being reinstated, eventually terminating on the far side of the town. The town's first gasworks was close to the canal; the one shown was completed in 1866 and was annually consuming over 1000 tons of coal by 1900. The figure was 2500 by the time of closure in 1960.

Coal Wharf

Jubilee Siding

Timber Yard

Timber Wharf

F.B.

Tank

P

F.B.

SEVERN ROAD

S.P Sl

Gas Works

59.　　This postcard view is thought to be from 1906. There were nine employees here in the 1930s. The building was still standing in 2009, serving commercial purposes. (Lens of Sutton coll.)

60.　　A northward view on 9th July 1949 contains no. 9002 with the 3.5pm from Oswestry and no. 9025 heading the 3.10pm from Shrewsbury. The locomotives are "Dukedog" 4-4-0s. The trains would be joined here and arrive at Aberystwyth at 6.0pm. (W.A.Camwell/SLS coll.)

61.   Standing at the bay platform on 30th June 1956 is the 12.25pm to Whitchurch. It is headed by no. 9017, another "Dukekdog". (H.C.Casserley)

**Other views of Welshpool can be seen in
pictures 64 to 77 in *Shrewsbury to Newtown*
and 1 to 52 in *Welshpool to Llanfair*.
The latter features the narrow gauge line through the town.**

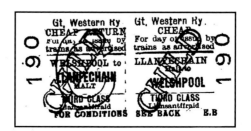

62.　　A 1959 panorama has the 6-ton crane on the right, but the water tower obscures the turntable and engine shed. The latter housed only one locomotive and closed in 1954. On the right is 4-6-0 no. 7814 *Fringford Manor*. (R.G.Nelson/T.Walsh)

63.　　No. 7812 *Erlestoke Manor* stands with the 12.35pm Aberystwyth to Crewe via Oswestry on 31st March 1962, while 2-6-0 no. 7336 waits on the right to leave with the rear coaches for Shrewsbury at 3.20. The former is preserved on the Severn Valley Railway. The tracks and platforms were removed in 1992 to make way for a bypass. A loop, with an island platform, was created further north. (H.Ballantyne)

2. Tanat Valley Branch
PORTHYWAEN

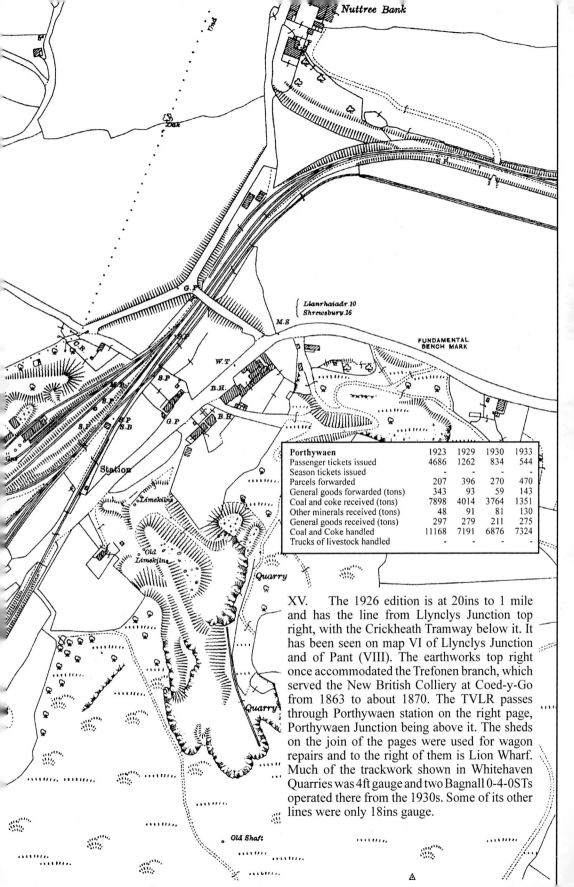

Nuttree Bank

Und

Oak

G.F.

M.S

Llanrhaiadr 10
Shrewsbury 16

FUNDAMENTAL
BENCH MARK

C.R.

W.T.

B.P.

B.H.

M.R.

B.P.

S.P.
S.B.

S.P.

B.H.

G.P.

Station

Limekilns

Old
Limekilns

Quarry

Quarry

Old Shaft

Porthywaen	1923	1929	1930	1933
Passenger tickets issued	4686	1262	834	544
Season tickets issued	-	-	-	-
Parcels forwarded	207	396	270	470
General goods forwarded (tons)	343	93	59	143
Coal and coke received (tons)	7898	4014	3764	1351
Other minerals received (tons)	48	91	81	130
General goods received (tons)	297	279	211	275
Coal and Coke handled	11168	7191	6876	7324
Trucks of livestock handled	-	-	-	-

XV.   The 1926 edition is at 20ins to 1 mile
and has the line from Llynclys Junction top
right, with the Crickheath Tramway below it. It
has been seen on map VI of Llynclys Junction
and of Pant (VIII). The earthworks top right
once accommodated the Trefonen branch, which
served the New British Colliery at Coed-y-Go
from 1863 to about 1870. The TVLR passes
through Porthywaen station on the right page,
Porthywaen Junction being above it. The sheds
on the join of the pages were used for wagon
repairs and to the right of them is Lion Wharf.
Much of the trackwork shown in Whitehaven
Quarries was 4ft gauge and two Bagnall 0-4-0STs
operated there from the 1930s. Some of its other
lines were only 18ins gauge.

64.   Bagnall 0-4-0ST no. 2 *Whitehaven* was photographed on the indifferent quality 4ft gauge track of Whitehaven Quarries on 2nd July 1949. (R.S.Carpenter coll.)

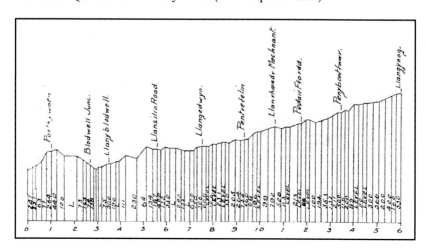

65.   This 1949 panorama has the ex-TVLR track to the left of Porthywaen signal box, together with the platform. The track behind the box was dual gauge in the early years and the map shows the tramway crossing the main line north of it. (R.S.Carpenter coll.)

66.   The bridge can be found on the map and under it, sometime in the late 1940s, is 0-6-0ST no. 1331. It had been built for the Whitland & Cardigan Railway. The bridge carries the Porthywaen branch over the line to Whitehaven Quarries. (D.K.Jones coll.)

67.   A 1948 northward view includes the box, which only served as a ground frame. It had 12 levers; the branch is beyond. (R.S.Carpenter coll.)

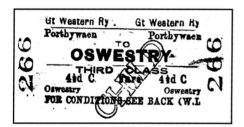

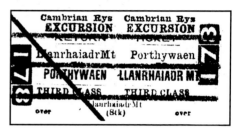

68.   The relationship of the main road (A495 since 1919) to the platform and the box was recorded on 20th September 1958. The oil lamp has a red glass to warn road users of the presence of the crossing. (H.C.Casserley)

69.   Seen on 12th March 1966, a train creeps across the deserted road. Note that the gates did not swing across the road, but there is a warning sign on the verge. (A.M.Davies)

70.   A northward view on the same day was taken while the train stood to allow its guard to close the gates. (A.M.Davies)

LLANDDU JUNCTION

71.   This is where the Nantmawr branch left the Tanat Valley route. The view east is from 1948 and has the line to Nantmawr Quarry and Llanddu Quarry on the left. The 1904 connection for the TVLR is on the right. (R.S.Carpenter coll.)

72.   Running onto the branch on 12th March 1966 is 2-6-0 no. 46514. The milepost records 2¼ miles from Llynclys Junction. (A.M.Davies)

73.　A new stone loading facility was built close to the site of the junction in about 1980 and the remaining spur to Llanddu Quarry was taken out of use. No. 25052 is arriving with empty wagons from Bescot on 21st August 1985 and has just run under the lane to the quarry and Blodwell Hall. All rail traffic from Gobowen ceased on 28th October 1989, but official closure was not until 3rd October 1993. The equipment was dismantled in 2008. (P.D.Shannon)

Nantmawr	1923	1929	1930	1933
General goods forwarded (tons)	5	-	-	-
Coal and coke received (tons)	623	494	1038	147
Other minerals received (tons)	-	-	178	-
General goods received (tons)	27	-	85	12
Coal and Coke handled	861	-	-	77
Trucks of livestock handled	-	-	-	-

NANTMAWR

74.　The branch passed under the A495 before reaching the quarry, seen here in 1961. Stone trains ran to Nantmawr Quarry until 21st October 1971, reversing at Blodwell Junction. (A.M.Davies)

BLODWELL JUNCTION

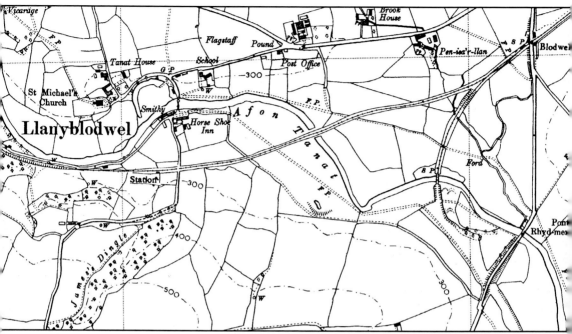

XVI. The 1949 revision at 6ins to 1 mile has the A495 running almost vertically on the right and passing over the station. Running across the map is the former TVLR and curving south from it is a siding on the alignment of the "Potts".

75. The station was initially called "Llanyblodwell" and it is seen prior to rebuilding, renaming and reopening by the TVLR in 1904. (R.S.Carpenter coll.)

76.   A 1904 photograph includes the then new signal box, platform and loop provided by the TVLR. The bridge had been built by the "Potts". The nearest building contained the gents and the lamp room. The signal box had 20 levers. The road bridge was supported by brick columns after line closure. (R.S.Carpenter coll.)

77.   A TVLR train runs close to a wagon standing in the loop, which was used by locomotives running round trains on the Llanymynech-Llangynog service in the 1904-15 period. Trains from the former then terminated here until withdrawn two years later. (R.S.Carpenter coll.)

Blodwell Junction	1923	1929	1930	1933
Passenger tickets issued	3437	1962	1374	1086
Season tickets issued	1	-	-	1
Parcels forwarded	1021	3060	7101	225
General goods forwarded (tons)	18	140	5	4
Coal and coke received (tons)	-	435	283	306
Other minerals received (tons)	298	65	53	495
General goods received (tons)	482	238	308	142
Coal and Coke handled	462	302	102	254
Trucks of livestock handled	-	-	-	-

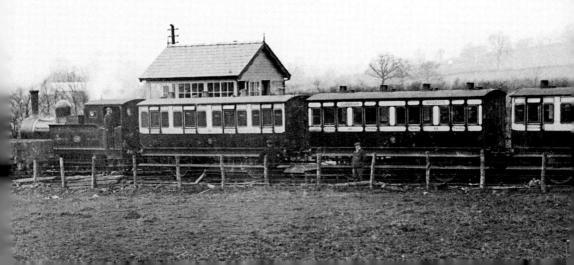

78.   This panorama from the road bridge is from October 1931 and has the original line from Llanymynech curving left at the junction in the distance. Behind the camera, there was a short goods siding on the north side of the line, in use until 6th January 1964. (R.S.Carpenter coll.)

79.   A close up of the junction in 1948 includes the loop. The line on the right carried a passenger service to Llanymynech until 1917. The line was severed in 1925. The GWR provided three men here, prior to World War II. (R.S.Carpenter coll.)

LLANYBLODWELL

80.   The station was opened in 1904 west of the village, which had a steady population: 795 in 1901 and 768 in 1961. There was a goods loop on the north side of the line until May 1941. This early view includes a white-painted urinal at the far end of the platform. The station is marked on the previous map, towards the left. (R.S.Carpenter coll.)

GLANYRAFON

81.   This view towards Blodwell Junction is from 1963. There was a footpath over the fields and across a footbridge over the Tanat. The halt opened on 1st September 1904. (C.C.Green)

LLANSILIN ROAD

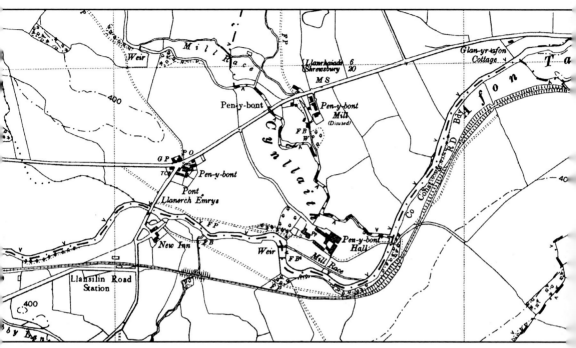

XVII. The station is lower left on this 1949 extract at 6 ins to 1 mile. Montgomeryshire is south of the River Tanat, while Shropshire is to the right of the Cynllaith and Denbighshire is to the left of it. The county boundary deviates, so that the latter county included the stations at Llangedwyn and Pentrefelin.

82.　　　There was one man employed here in the 1930s. The goods loop and shed were on the north side of the line, but only the latter is shown on the map, although goods traffic is recorded as discontinued on 6th January 1964. The photograph is from 1961. (A.M.Davies)

Llansilin Road	1923	1929	1930	1933
Passenger tickets issued	3767	3122	2327	2598
Season tickets issued	-	-	1	-
Parcels forwarded	889	1569	2747	297
General goods forwarded (tons)	577	37	114	32
Coal and coke received (tons)	36	128	199	231
Other minerals received (tons)	333	213	938	168
General goods received (tons)	1006	619	485	161
Coal and Coke handled	1249	951	947	642
Trucks of livestock handled	76	141	83	75

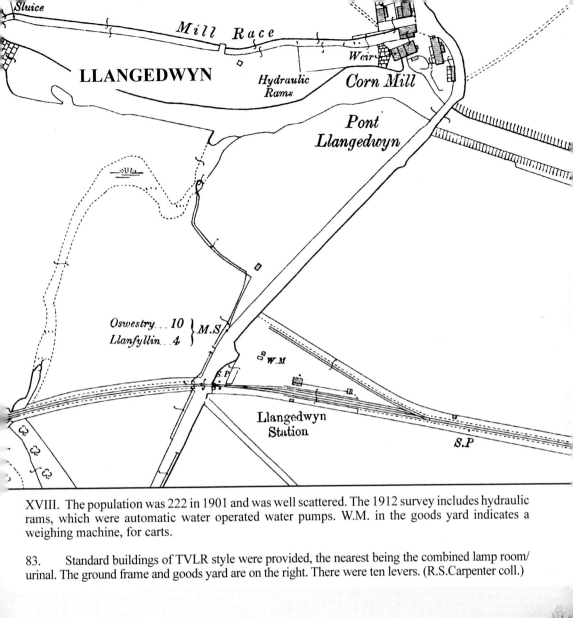

Map labels:

Sluice

Mill Race

Weir

LLANGEDWYN

Hydraulic Rams

Corn Mill

Pont Llangedwyn

Oswestry ... 10 } M.S
Llanfyllin ... 4 }

W.M

S.P

Llangedwyn Station

S.P

XVIII. The population was 222 in 1901 and was well scattered. The 1912 survey includes hydraulic rams, which were automatic water operated water pumps. W.M. in the goods yard indicates a weighing machine, for carts.

83.   Standard buildings of TVLR style were provided, the nearest being the combined lamp room/urinal. The ground frame and goods yard are on the right. There were ten levers. (R.S.Carpenter coll.)

84.   The GWR disconnected the loop, but retained both platforms. Westbound in the late 1940s is 0-4-2T no. 5812. The white patch on the left is where the platform had been raised for cattle traffic. (Lens of Sutton coll.)

85.   The goods yard closed on 2nd May 1949, but one siding was retained for wagon storage, as recorded on 20th September 1958. There was a solitary employee in the 1930s. (H.C.Casserley)

WEST OF LLANGEDWYN

86.   The bridge over the River Tanat is seen in about 1904 and one abutment foundation was eroded on 4th December 1960. This brought total closure westwards. (R.S.Carpenter coll.)

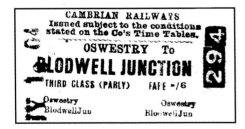

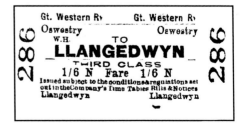

PENTREFELIN

87.   The original track can be examined in this 1904 westward view. The goods loop was in use until 16th May 1941. (R.S.Carpenter coll.)

XIX. T.C. refers to Travelling Crane. The map is from 1912.

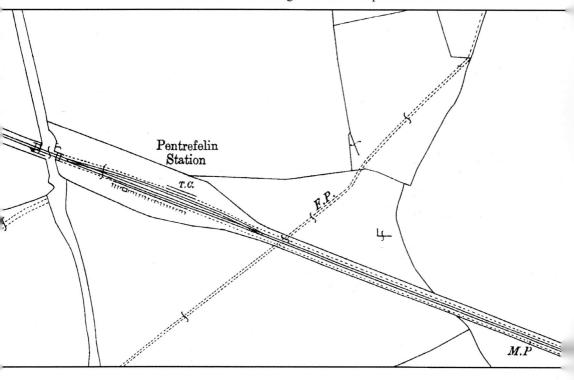

Pentrefelin
Station

T.C.

F.P.

M.P

LLANRHAIADR MOCHNANT

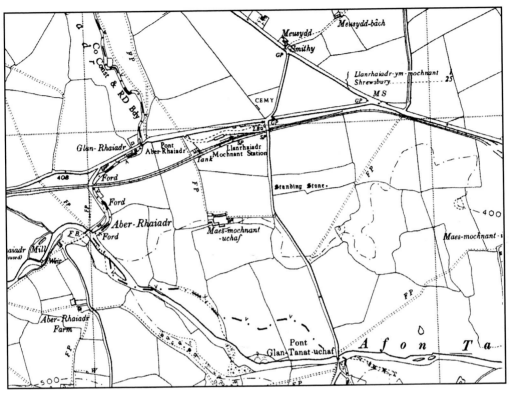

XX.   The 1949 edition at 6ins to 1 mile shows the remote location of the station, plus the dots and dashes of the county boundary.

88.   Departing for Oswestry in June 1947 is 2-4-0T no. 1197. It is about to pass over the ungated level crossing at the east end of the station site. (M.Whitehouse coll.)

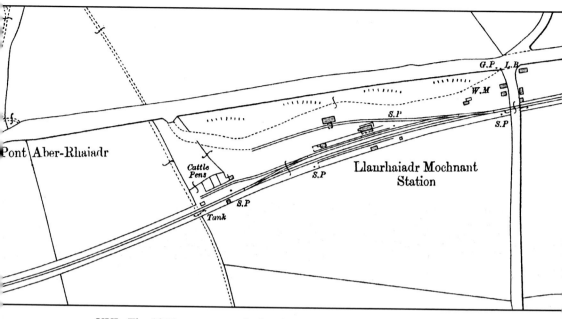

Pont Aber-Rhaiadr

Cattle Pens

S.P

Tank

S.P

S.P

Llaurhaiadr Mochnant Station

S.P

W.M

G.P. L.B

S.P

XXI. The 1912 survey reveals that there were cattle pens from an early date.

89.   We are at the west of the station in 1958 to see the tank, its pump shed and the cattle dock. There was an open ground frame with 12 levers. (A.M.Davies)

90.   We now have three photographs from 20th September 1958, which record what seems to be the only train to carry passengers since 1951. We are at the east end. There was a staff of two recorded in 1923-38. (R.M.Casserley)

91.   Moving closer and up a signal post, the two nearest vans appear to be out of use, but two coal wagons are open for unloading. (R.M.Casserley)

92.   The tour operator becomes apparent, as does 2-6-0 no. 46509 and probably the only remaining urinal on the route by that time. (G.Adams/M.J.Stretton coll.)

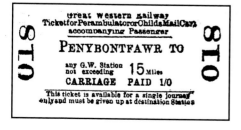

018   018

Great Western Railway
Ticket for Perambulator or Childs Mail Car,
accompanying Passenger

PENYBONTFAWR TO

any G.W. Station   15 Miles
not exceeding

CARRIAGE PAID 1/0

This ticket is available for a single journey
only and must be given up at destination Stations

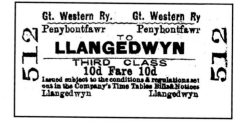

512   512

Gt. Western Ry.   Gt. Western Ry
Penybontfawr   Penybontfawr
TO
LLANGEDWYN
THIRD CLASS
10d Fare 10d
Issued subject to the conditions & regulations set
out in the Company's Time Tables Bills & Notices
Llangedwyn   Llangedwyn

PEDAIR FFORDD HALT

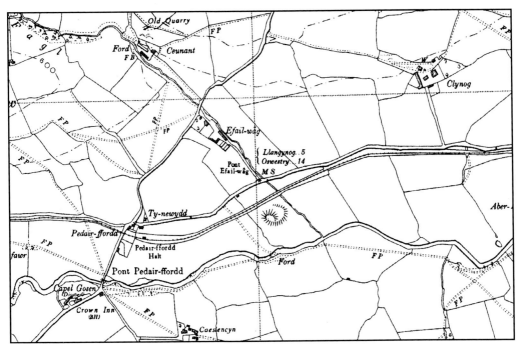

XXIII. The 1949 map at 6ins to 1 mile again shows sparse population. West of the halt is the B4396, which the line passed over on an ungated crossing.

93.   A timber platform, a small shed and two lamps sufficed at this remote location. This is a 1904 photograph. (R.S.Carpenter coll.)

PENYBONTFAWR

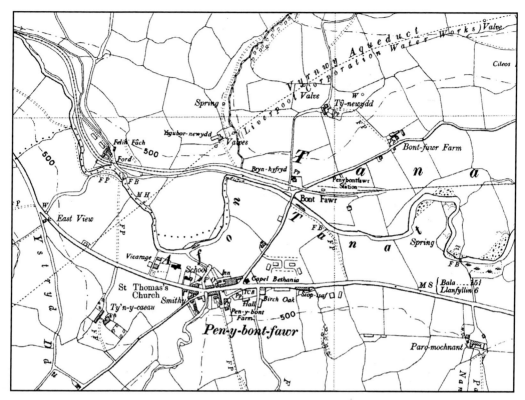

XXIV. The 6ins to 1 mile survey of 1949 shows a compact village and the line following the winding course of the river. The railway passed over the aqueduct pipeline on a stone bridge.

94.   The Tanat Valley narrows as it reaches almost 500ft above sea level. This is a 1904 view westwards. The yard was equipped with a weighing machine for road vehicles. (R.S.Carpenter coll.)

95.   The goods yard closed on 1st July 1952 and was photographed on 3rd November 1956. Much timber had been loaded here in times gone by. (A.M.Davies)

CAMBRIAN RAILWAYS
Issued subject to the Conditions
stated in the Co's Time Tables

LLANGYNOG To
PEDAIR FFORDD

476

THIRD CLASS   REVISED FARE ·/4

CHILD

CAMBRIAN RAILWAYS
Issued subject to the Conditions
stated in the Co's Time Tables

LLANGYNOG To
PORTHYWAEN

THIRD CLASS   REVISED FARE 2/2½
Llangynog   Llangynog
Porthywaen   Porthywaen

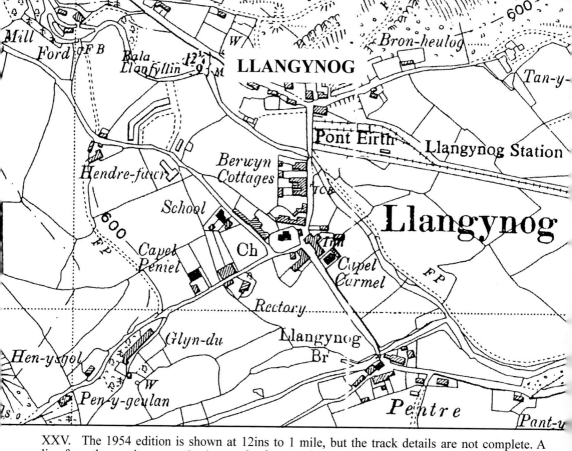

XXV. The 1954 edition is shown at 12ins to 1 mile, but the track details are not complete. A line from the granite quarry (top) to a wharf, west of the road near the station, had long gone. The population fell from 514 in 1901 to 292 in 1961.

96. Ready to return to Oswestry sometime in the 1930s are two four-wheeled coaches, hauled by ex-CR 0-6-0 no. 908. The GWR provided three men from 1923 to 1932 and two thereafter. (R.S.Carpenter coll.)

97.　　A panorama from 5th July 1941 includes the 1906 slate storage area, which is a light colour on the right. The nearest line of coaches are berthed. The locomotive is ex-CR 2-4-0T no. 1196. (R.E.Tustin/R.S.Carpenter coll.)

98.　　We finish our visit to the Tanat Valley with two pictures from November 1956, four years after traffic had ceased. Goods and passenger buildings were still complete and the nine-lever ground frame stood sentinel over the site. (A.M.Davies)

99.　　The line in the foreground had once passed over a level crossing to reach the wharf for granite, while the one with the pit had earlier served an engine shed. The water tank had been on the right. (A.M.Davies)

3. Llanfyllin Branch
CARREGHOFA HALT

100.   We go to the western edge of Llanymynech to find this halt, which opened on 11th April 1938. The nearest bridge carries the A490, while the further one is for the Shropshire Union Canal. (C.C.Green)

101.   A view from the road, looking east, is from December 1964. The halt was open until line closure. The location is shown on map I. (A.M.Davies)

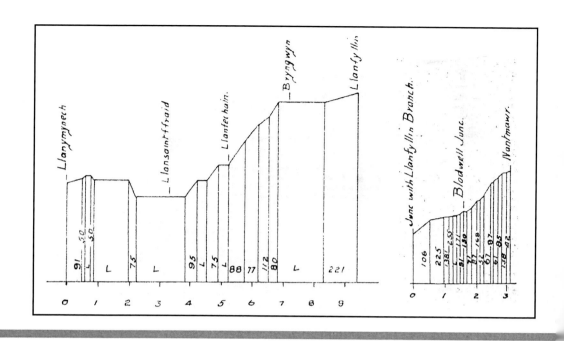

NANTMAWR JUNCTION

102. This 1904 westward view has the Llanfyllin branch on the left and the line north to Nantmawr on the right. The 1904 box had 13 levers and closed in April 1917, when the link north became two long storage sidings. This was known as Wern junction in the days of "The Potts". (R.S.Carpenter coll.)

LLANSANTFFRAID

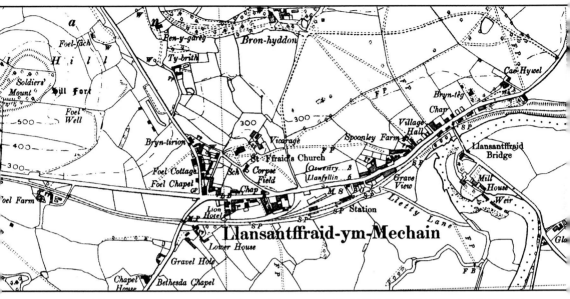

XXVI. The 1949 edition at 6ins to 1 mile has the A490 running close to the branch, through the village.

103.   The dimensions of the chimney pot make an interesting comparison with those of the underclothes. The box opened on 9th January 1893 and its 14-lever frame was in use until line closure. (P.J.Garland/ R.S.Carpenter)

104. The signalman is seen from a westbound train on 14th September 1956. There were five men listed in the 1930s. The building became a tourist centre in 1969 and was a restaurant subsequently. (R.M.Casserley)

→ 105. An eastward panorama from November 1964 includes the goods shed, which contained a crane of one-ton capacity. Goods traffic ceased that month. (R.G.Nelson/T.Walsh)

→ 106. The goods yard was recorded in the other direction, plus the cattle feed mill, a few days later. The foothills of the Cambrian Mountains are in the background. (A.M.Davies)

LLANFECHAIN

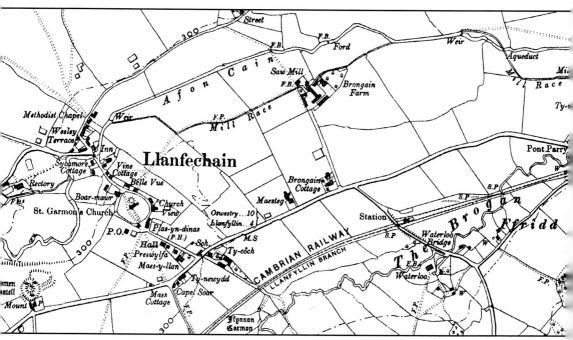

XXVII. The 1938 survey at 6ins to 1 mile includes the entire village, which housed 394 souls in 1901.

107. The station had to share the men listed at the terminus. The photograph is from 14th September 1956. (R.M.Casserley)

108.   A six-lever ground frame was listed until 1929, but a smaller one sufficed until the goods yard closed on 27th July 1964. A westbound train and 2-6-0 no. 46512 are pictured from the bridge in about 1962. (D.Wilson)

BRYNGWYN

109.   The original timber structure was replaced with concrete slabs and they were photographed in September 1956. Timetables suggest that opening was in May 1865 and full use was from June 1867. (R.M.Casserley)

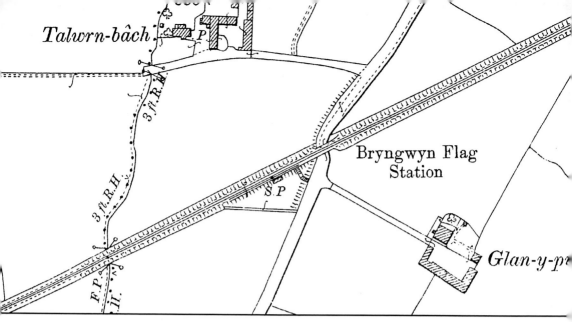

Talwrn-bâch

Bryngwyn Flag Station

Glan-y-p

XXVIII. The 1901 survey makes it clear that this was a request stop, but it was on certain days only for the first years, usually Wednesday and Thursday.

110.   It is December 1964 and we look towards Llanymynech from an departing train, as the sun sets. On the right are the steps down to the road. (A.M.Davies)

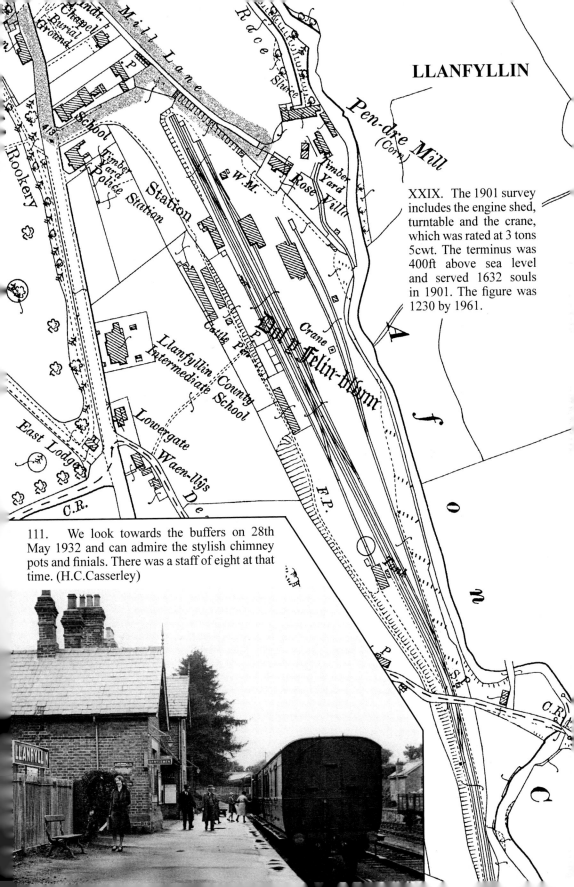

LLANFYLLIN

XXIX. The 1901 survey includes the engine shed, turntable and the crane, which was rated at 3 tons 5cwt. The terminus was 400ft above sea level and served 1632 souls in 1901. The figure was 1230 by 1961.

111. We look towards the buffers on 28th May 1932 and can admire the stylish chimney pots and finials. There was a staff of eight at that time. (H.C.Casserley)

LLANFYLLIN

112. An April 1938 view from the end of the line includes a 0-4-2T and a horse box in the shadows, while a luxury motor car awaits a passenger or two. (D.K.Jones coll.)

113. Camping coaches became popular with the advent of holidays with pay in the 1930s. One is pictured in 1939, but the GWR term is seen to be CAMP COACH. (Speight coll.)

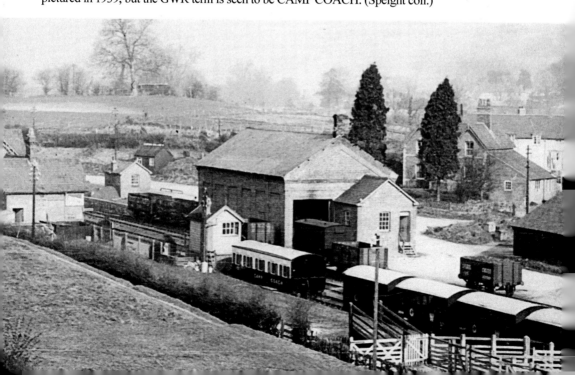

114.   The locomotive is part way along its train in this view from the 1950s. It was unusual to find just a few concrete sleepers. (R.G.Nelson/T.Walsh)

115.   Recorded on 21st May 1953 is the 1863 engine shed, which was in use until 1952. In its final years, it usually housed one 0-4-2T. The GWR code was OSW and BR used 89A, a sub shed to Oswestry. (P.J.Garland/R.S.Carpenter)

116.   The end of the line was photographed on 14th September 1956 as 0-6-0PT no. 7410 is about to change direction. (R.M.Casserley)

117.   The same locomotive is departing on 3rd November 1956 and we can examine a traditional CR signal post. The ringed arm was for shunting movements. (A.M.Davies)

118.   The SLS railtour on 20th September 1958 has been seen on the Tanat Valley branch in picture no. 92. The locomotive is 2-6-0 no. 46509 and also appears in photograph 17. (G.Adams/M.J.Stretton coll.)

119.   Two more of the same class were recorded in about 1962. No. 46512 waits with a passenger train, while no. 46511 is coupled to a freight, both destined for Oswestry. (D. Wilson)

120.   The final view is from 12th November 1964, ten days after freight traffic had ceased. The 1892 signal box had 14 levers and was functional to the end. The coal office and store is on the left. In the background is Green Hall Hill, one of many which enhanced the journey on the branch. (R.G. Nelson/T. Walsh)

MP Middleton Press

EVOLVING THE ULTIMATE RAIL ENCYCLOPEDIA

Easebourne Lane, Midhurst, West Sussex.
GU29 9AZ   Tel:01730 813169
www.middletonpress.co.uk   email:info@middletonpress.co.uk
A-978 0 906520 B- 978 1 873793 C- 978 1 901706 D-978 1 904474
E - 978 1 906008 F - 978 1 908174

All titles listed below were in print at time of publication - please check current availability by looking at our
website - *www.middletonpress.co.uk* or by requesting a Brochure which includes our
LATEST RAILWAY TITLES also our TRAMWAY, TROLLEYBUS, MILITARY and COASTAL series

A

Abergavenny to Merthyr C 91 8
Abertillery & Ebbw Vale Lines D 84 5
Aberystwyth to Carmarthen E 90 1
Allhallows - Branch Line to A 62 8
Alton - Branch Lines to A 11 6
Andover to Southampton A 82 6
Ascot - Branch Lines around A 64 2
Ashburton - Branch Line to B 95 4
Ashford - Steam to Eurostar B 67 1
Ashford to Dover A 48 2
Austrian Narrow Gauge D 04 3
Avonmouth - BL around D 42 5
Aylesbury to Rugby D 91 3

B

Baker Street to Uxbridge D 90 6
Bala to Llandudno E 87 1
Banbury to Birmingham D 27 2
Banbury to Cheltenham E 63 5
Bangor to Holyhead F 01 7
Bangor to Portmadoc E 72 7
Barking to Southend C 80 2
Barmouth to Pwllheli E 53 6
Barry - Branch Lines around D 50 0
Bartlow - Branch Lines to F 27 7
Bath Green Park to Bristol C 36 9
Bath to Evercreech Junction A 60 4
Beamish 40 years on rails E94 9
Bedford to Wellingborough D 31 9
Berwick to Drem F 64 2
Berwick to St. Boswells F 75 8
B'ham to Tamworth & Nuneaton F 63 5
Birkenhead to West Kirby F 61 1
Birmingham to Wolverhampton E253
Bletchley to Cambridge D 94 4
Bletchley to Rugby E 07 9
Bodmin - Branch Lines around B 83 1
Bournemouth to Evercreech Jn A 46 8
Bournemouth to Weymouth A 57 4
Bradshaw's Guide 1866 F 05 5
Bradshaw's History F18 5
Bradshaw's Rail Times 1850 F 13 0
Bradshaw's Rail Times 1895 F 11 6
Branch Lines series - see town names
Brecon to Neath D 43 2
Brecon to Newport D 16 6
Brecon to Newtown E 06 2
Brighton to Eastbourne A 16 1
Brighton to Worthing A 03 1
Bristol to Taunton D 03 6
Bromley South to Rochester B 23 7
Bromsgrove to Birmingham D 87 6
Bromsgrove to Gloucester D 73 9
Broxbourne to Cambridge F16 1
Brunel - A railtour D 74 6
Bude - Branch Line to B 29 9
Burnham to Evercreech Jn B 68 0

C

Cambridge to Ely D 55 5
Canterbury - BLs around B 58 9
Cardiff to Dowlais (Cae Harris) E 47 5
Cardiff to Pontypridd E 95 6
Cardiff to Swansea E 42 0
Carlisle to Hawick E 85 7
Carmarthen to Fishguard E 66 6
Caterham & Tattenham Corner B251
Central & Southern Spain NG E 91 8
Chard and Yeovil - BLs a C 30 7
Charing Cross to Dartford A 75 8
Charing Cross to Orpington A 96 3
Cheddar - Branch Line to B 90 9
Cheltenham to Andover C 43 7
Cheltenham to Redditch D 81 4
Chester to Birkenhead F 21 5
Chester to Manchester F 51 2
Chester to Rhyl E 93 2
Chester to Warrington F 40 6
Chichester to Portsmouth A 14 7
Clacton and Walton - BLs to F 04 8
Clapham Jn to Beckenham Jn B 36 7

Cleobury Mortimer - BLs a E 18 5
Clevedon & Portishead - BLs to D180
Consett to South Shields E 57 4
Cornwall Narrow Gauge D 56 2
Corris and Vale of Rheidol E 65 9
Craven Arms to Llandeilo E 35 2
Craven Arms to Wellington E 33 8
Crawley to Littlehampton A 34 5
Crewe to Manchester F 57 4
Cromer - Branch Lines around C 26 0
Croydon to East Grinstead B 48 0
Crystal Palace & Catford Loop B 87 1
Cyprus Narrow Gauge E 13 0

D

Darjeeling Revisited F 09 3
Darlington Leamside Newcastle E 28 4
Darlington to Newcastle D 98 2
Dartford to Sittingbourne B 34 3
Denbigh - Branch Lines around F 32 1
Derwent Valley - BL to the D 06 7
Devon Narrow Gauge E 09 3
Didcot to Banbury D 02 9
Didcot to Swindon C 84 0
Didcot to Winchester C 13 0
Dorset & Somerset NG D 76 0
Douglas - Laxey - Ramsey E 75 8
Douglas to Peel C 88 8
Douglas to Port Erin C 55 0
Douglas to Ramsey D 39 5
Dover to Ramsgate A 78 9
Dublin Northwards in 1950s E 31 4
Dunstable - Branch Lines to E 27 7

E

Ealing to Slough C 42 0
Eastbourne to Hastings A 27 7
East Cornwall Mineral Railways D 22 7
East Croydon to Three Bridges A 53 6
Eastern Spain Narrow Gauge E 56 7
East Grinstead - BLs to A 07 9
East London - Branch Lines of C 44 4
East London Line B 80 0
East of Norwich - Branch Lines E 69 7
Effingham Junction - BLs a A 74 1
Ely to Norwich C 90 1
Enfield Town & Palace Gates D 32 6
Epsom to Horsham A 30 7
Eritrean Narrow Gauge E 38 3
Euston to Harrow & Wealdstone C 89 5
Exeter to Barnstaple B 15 2
Exeter to Newton Abbot C 49 9
Exeter to Tavistock B 69 5
Exmouth - Branch Lines to B 00 8

F

Fairford - Branch Line to A 52 9
Falmouth, Helston & St. Ives C 74 1
Fareham to Salisbury A 67 3
Faversham to Dover B 05 3
Felixstowe & Aldeburgh - BL to D 20 3
Fenchurch Street to Barking C 20 8
Festiniog - 50 yrs of enterprise C 83 3
Festiniog 1946-55 E 01 7
Festiniog in the Fifties B 68 8
Festiniog in the Sixties B 91 6
Ffestiniog in Colour 1955-82 F 25 3
Finsbury Park to Alexandra Pal C 02 8
Frome to Bristol B 77 0

G

Galashiels to Edinburgh F 52 9
Gloucester to Bristol D 35 7
Gloucester to Cardiff D 66 1
Gosport - Branch Lines around A 36 9
Greece Narrow Gauge D 72 2

H

Hampshire Narrow Gauge D 36 4
Harrow to Watford D 14 2
Harwich & Hadleigh - BLs to F 02 4
Harz Revisited F 62 8
Hastings to Ashford A 37 6
Hawick to Galashiels F 36 9

Hawkhurst - Branch Line to A 66 6
Hayling - Branch Line to A 12 3
Hay-on-Wye - BL around D 92 0
Haywards Heath to Seaford A 28 4
Hemel Hempstead - BLs to D 88 3
Henley, Windsor & Marlow - BLa C77 2
Hereford to Newport D 54 8
Hertford & Hatfield - BLs a E 58 1
Hertford Loop E 71 0
Hexham to Carlisle D 75 3
Hexham to Hawick F 08 6
Hitchin to Peterborough D 07 4
Holborn Viaduct to Lewisham A 81 9
Horsham - Branch Lines to A 02 4
Huntingdon - Branch Line to A 93 2

I

Ilford to Shenfield C 97 0
Ilfracombe - Branch Line to B 21 3
Industrial Rlys of the South East A 09 3
Ipswich to Saxmundham C 41 3
Isle of Wight Lines - 50 yrs C 12 3
Italy Narrow Gauge F 17 8

K

Kent Narrow Gauge C 45 1
Kidderminster to Shrewsbury E 10 9
Kingsbridge - Branch Line to C 98 7
Kings Cross to Potters Bar E 62 8
King's Lynn to Hunstanton F 58 1
Kingston & Hounslow Loops A 83 3
Kingswear - Branch Line to C 17 8

L

Lambourn - Branch Line to C 70 3
Launceston & Princetown - BLs C 19 2
Lewisham to Dartford A 92 5
Lincoln to Cleethorpes F 56 7
Lines around Wimbledon B 75 6
Liverpool Street to Chingford D 01 2
Liverpool Street to Ilford C 34 5
Llandeilo to Swansea E 46 8
London Bridge to Addiscombe B 20 6
London Bridge to East Croydon A 58 1
Longmoor - Branch Lines to A 41 3
Looe - Branch Line to C 22 2
Loughborough to Nottingham F 68 0
Lowestoft - BLs around E 40 6
Ludlow to Hereford E 14 7
Lydney - Branch Lines around E 26 0
Lyme Regis - Branch Line to A 45 1
Lynton - Branch Line to B 04 6

M

Machynlleth to Barmouth E 54 3
Maesteg and Tondu Lines E 06 2
Majorca & Corsica Narrow Gauge F 41 3
March - Branch Lines around B 09 1
Market Drayton - Branch around F 67 3
Marylebone to Rickmansworth D 49 4
Melton Constable to Yarmouth Bch E031
Midhurst - Branch Lines of E 78 9
Midhurst - Branch Lines to F 00 0
Minehead - Branch Line to A 80 2
Mitcham Junction Lines B 01 5
Monmouth - Branch Lines to E 20 8
Monmouthshire Eastern Valleys D 71 5
Moretonhampstead - BL to C 27 7
Moreton-in-Marsh to Worcester D 26 5
Mountain Ash to Neath D 80 7

N

Newbury to Westbury C 66 6
Newcastle to Hexham D 69 2
Newport (IOW) - Branch Lines A 26 0
Newquay - Branch Lines to C 71 0
Newton Abbot to Plymouth C 60 4
Newtown to Aberystwyth E 41 3
North East German NG D 44 9
Northern Alpine Narrow Gauge F 37 6
Northern France Narrow Gauge C 75 8
Northern Spain Narrow Gauge E 83 3
North London Line B 94 7
North of Birmingham F 55 0

North Woolwich - BLs around C 65 9
Nottingham to Boston F 70 3
Nottingham to Lincoln F 43 7

O

Ongar - Branch Line to E 05 5
Orpington to Tonbridge B 03 9
Oswestry - Branch Lines around E 60 4
Oswestry to Whitchurch E 81 9
Oxford to Bletchley D 57 9
Oxford to Moreton-in-Marsh D 15 9

P

Paddington to Ealing C 37 6
Paddington to Princes Risborough C819
Padstow - Branch Line to B 54 1
Pembroke and Cardigan - BLs to F 29 1
Peterborough to Kings Lynn E 32 1
Peterborough to Newark F 72 7
Plymouth - BLs around B 98 5
Plymouth to St. Austell C 63 5
Pontypool to Mountain Ash D 65 4
Pontypridd to Merthyr F 14 7
Pontypridd to Port Talbot E 86 4
Porthmadog 1954-94 - BLa B 31 2
Portmadoc 1923-46 - BLa B 13 8
Portsmouth to Southampton A 31 4
Portugal Narrow Gauge E 67 3
Potters Bar to Cambridge D 70 8
Princes Risborough - BL to D 05 0
Princes Risborough to Banbury C 85 7

R

Railways to Victory C 16 1
Reading to Basingstoke B 27 5
Reading to Didcot C 79 6
Redhill to Ashford A 73 4
Return to Blaenau 1970-82 C 64 2
Rhyl to Bangor F 15 4
Rhymney & New Tredegar Lines E 48 2
Rickmansworth to Aylesbury D 61 6
Romania & Bulgaria NG E 23 9
Romneyrail C 32 1
Ross-on-Wye - BLs around E 30 7
Ruabon to Barmouth E 84 0
Rugby to Birmingham E 37 6
Rugby to Loughborough F 12 3
Rugby to Stafford F 07 9
Ryde to Ventnor A 19 2

S

Salisbury to Westbury B 39 8
Sardinia and Sicily Narrow Gauge F 50 5
Saxmundham to Yarmouth C 69 7
Saxony & Baltic Germany Revisited F 71 0
Saxony Narrow Gauge D 47 0
Seaton & Sidmouth - BLs to A 95 6
Selsey - Branch Line to A 04 8
Sheerness - Branch Line to B 16 2
Shenfield to Ipswich E 96 3
Shrewsbury - Branch Line to A 86 4
Shrewsbury to Chester E 70 3
Shrewsbury to Crewe F 48 2
Shrewsbury to Ludlow E 21 5
Shrewsbury to Newtown E 29 1
Sierra Leone Narrow Gauge D 28 9
Sirhowy Valley Line E 12 3
Sittingbourne to Ramsgate A 90 1
Slough to Newbury C 56 7
South African Two-foot gauge E 51 2
Southampton to Bournemouth A 42 0
Southend & Southminster BLs E 76 5
Southern Alpine Narrow Gauge F 22 2
Southern France Narrow Gauge C 47 5
South London Line B 46 6
South Lynn to Norwich City F 03 1
Southwold - Branch Line to A 15 4
Spalding - Branch Lines around E 52 9
Spalding to Grimsby F 65 9 6
Stafford to Chester F 34 5
Stafford to Wellington F 59 8
St Albans to Bedford D 08 1

St. Austell to Penzance C 67 3
St. Boswell to Berwick F 44 4
Steaming Through Isle of Wig
Steaming Through West Hant
Stourbridge to Wolverhampto
St. Pancras to Barking D 68 5
St. Pancras to Folkestone E 8
St. Pancras to St. Albans C 7
Stratford to Cheshunt F 53 6
Stratford-u-Avon to Birmingha
Stratford-u-Avon to Cheltenha
Sudbury - Branch Lines to F
Surrey Narrow Gauge C 87 1
Sussex Narrow Gauge C 68 C
Swanley to Ashford B 45 9
Swansea - Branch Lines arou
Swansea to Carmarthen E 59
Swindon to Bristol C 96 3
Swindon to Gloucester D 46
Swindon to Newport D 30 2
Swiss Narrow Gauge C 94 9

T

Talyllyn 60 E 98 7
Tamworth to Derby F 76 5
Taunton to Barnstaple B 60 2
Taunton to Exeter C 82 6
Taunton to Minehead F 39 0
Tavistock to Plymouth B 88 6
Tenterden - Branch Line to A
Three Bridges to Brighton A 3
Tilbury Loop C 86 4
Tiverton - BLs around C 62 8
Tivetshall to Beccles D 41 8
Tonbridge to Hastings A 44 4
Torrington - Branch Lines to
Towcester - BLs around E 39
Tunbridge Wells BLs A 32 1

U

Upwell - Branch Line to B 64

V

Victoria to Bromley South A
Victoria to East Croydon A 4
Vivarais Revisited E 08 6

W

Walsall Routes F 45 1
Wantage - Branch Line to D 2
Wareham to Swanage 50 yrs
Waterloo to Windsor A 54 3
Waterloo to Woking A 38 3
Watford to Leighton Buzzard
Wellingborough to Leicester
Welshpool to Llanfair C 60 4
Wenford Bridge to Fowey C
Westbury to Bath B 55 8
Westbury to Taunton C 76 5
West Cornwall Mineral Rlys
West Croydon to Epsom B 0
West German Narrow Gauge
West London - BLs of C 50
West London Line B 84 8
West Wiltshire - BLs of D 12
Weymouth - BLs A 65 9
Willesden Jn to Richmond B
Wimbledon to Beckenham C
Wimbledon to Epsom B 62 6
Wimborne - BLs around A 9
Wisbech - BLs around C 01
Witham & Kelvedon - BLs a
Woking to Alton A 59 8
Woking to Portsmouth A 5
Woking to Southampton A 5
Wolverhampton to Shrewsb
Worcester to Birmingham D
Worcester to Hereford D 38
Worthing to Chichester A 06
Wrexham to New Brighton F
Wroxham - BLs around F 31

Y

Yeovil - 50 yrs change C 38
Yeovil to Dorchester A 76 5
Yeovil to Exeter A 91 8
York to Scarborough F 23 9